INFORMAL SOCIOLOGY

STUDIES IN
SOCIOLOGY

INFORMAL
SOCIOLOGY

*A
casual
introduction to
sociological thinking*

William Bruce Cameron
Bradley University

RANDOM HOUSE

NEW YORK

EDITOR'S FOREWORD

I first read most of the essays in this Study during a return flight from a four-day meeting of a national sociological society. The conclave had been the usual hectic affair: talking shop in bits and snatches with fellow-sociologists; inadvertently conducting field work in committee meetings led by current captains of the sociological establishment; visiting smoke-filled rooms where, as usual, much of the talk was a disorderly critique of that establishment; trying to hear at least a few promising papers without sabotaging those informal activities which are an essential, though unplanned, feature of such meetings. Reading Professor Cameron's essays relaxed the pace, but this was another reminder that informal "asides" can be sociologically instructive.

The informal essay—unsupported by rigorous use of empirical data, unmarked by theoretical ratiocination—runs counter to the present-day main drift of sociology, especially in the United States. But this mode of essay has been a persistent feature of both American and European sociology, reaching a high point of intellectual attainment in part of the work of such otherwise dissimilar writers as Georg Simmel and Thorstein Veblen in earlier years and Edward A. Shils and David Riesman today. Moreover, a sign of the growing maturity of sociology and of the professional self-confidence of its practitioners—some of Riesman's essays are a case in point—is the increasing number of light-hearted departures from the altogether serious business of sociological scholarship. Cameron's sallies into several segments of contemporary social and cultural life, including the booming sociological enterprise itself, illustrate this trend.

These essays afford some chuckles, to be sure, but they also provide heartier fare. Here are perceptive discussions of such matters of sociological concern as knowledge *with* and "without numbers," the role of physical surroundings in intellectual socialization, neglected aspects of social mobility, and that ubiquitous subject, jazz. (Several able sociologists are or have been jazz musicians—an example perhaps of "upward skidding"?) In his concluding essays Cameron turns to "cosmic" questions about contemporary life. For example, he considers the nature and foibles of "conservatives" and "liberals," and even presents a paradigm for the analysis of man, objects, and thought. His final plea for a "reasoned, consistent theory of the relations of people, things, and ideas" indicates the important and sober aim of the author of this less than sober book.

I suspect that Professor Cameron enjoyed writing these essays. Enjoyment and stimulation, I believe, are in store for sociological neophytes, graybeards of the field, and other readers of this *Informal Sociology*.

Charles H. Page

CONTENTS

ASSORTED SOCIAL PSYCHOLOGY

SAME OLD JAZZ

LET'S GET COSMIC

It is argued that basic values involve the relations of these three, that the possible relations are many, and that in our society we
falsely attribute the characteristics of each
to the others.

PREFACE

This is a collection of essays which I wrote just because I wanted to write them, "for kicks." Somewhat to my surprise, Random House wanted to publish them. I hope they find no reason to regret it. In these pages there is a small handful of original ideas, but most of the material has long been in intellectual public domain. The debt for some of it is uncollectable and goes back as far as Aristotle. More recent aid has come from a number of readers whom I was able to impose upon because they were friends. They deserve more than mere thanks, but that at least they shall receive. They include Ray Wheeler, who helped write one of the essays, Kalman Goldberg, Fred Ellwood, Robin Linstromberg, the late C. Wright Mills, Roy Francis, and my wife, C'Mari Cameron, each of whom has read and criticized one or more of the pieces printed here. Several publishers of journals have kindly consented to republication of work they first published, and these are noted with the essays which so appeared. Charles H. Page has been a helpful editor, and my students have been a handy captive audience.

Wm. Bruce Cameron
PEORIA, ILLINOIS
1963

Theory
and Methods

THE ELEMENTS
OF
STATISTICAL CONFUSION

Or: What Does
the Mean Mean?*

Scientific writers assure us that mathematics is rapidly becoming the language of all the sciences. In my own field, sociology, a casual survey of the journals shows that it already competes strongly with sociologese, which is an argot singularly difficult to displace. In any field which strives for impartiality and objectivity in its descriptions of nature, the cool and dispassionate language of numbers has its appeals, but statistics, that promising younger daughter of mathematics, is constantly threatened with seductions into easy virtue hardly matched since the *Perils of Pauline*.

The basic value and potential fault of numbers is that they are remote from reality, abstract, and aloof from the loose, qualitative differences which immediately impinge upon our senses. Numerous selections,

* Reprinted from the *Bulletin* of the American Association of University Professors (Vol. 43, Spring 1957) by permission.

generalizations, and discriminations take place before any aspect of sense experience can be reduced to a number, and most of the time we are hardly aware of these abstractions even as we make them. The simplest and most basic statistical operation is counting, which means that we can identify something clearly enough so that we can recognize it when we meet it again and keep track of the number of such events which occur. This sounds simple enough until we actually try to count objects, such as, let us say, students in various colleges in the university. It is easy enough to simply count everyone who enrolls, but deans, board members, and newspaper reporters want to know how many there are in various divisions. Suppose a student is finishing his undergraduate work and taking a few graduate courses as well. Is he one undergraduate, one graduate, or one of each? If someone takes a single course in evening college, is he then one evening student, or only one-fifth of a student? (Remember, we are trying to keep our private passions out of this description!) How many times he should be counted obviously depends on what it is we are trying to count, and for administrative purposes it may be best to count his *appearance* in each of these divisions; but unfortunately, any public listing of 5000 appearances is very likely to be interpreted as 5000 skinsful of student body, whereas we might find only 3000 epidermal units, or if you prefer clichés, 3000 noses. Equally obvious, 100 evening college students taking one two-hour course each are in no meaningful way equivalent to 100 day students, each with a sixteen hour load. The moral is: Not everything that can be counted counts.

If we have counted things to our satisfaction, we can express the numerical value of one class of objects in terms of the number of some other, as a fraction or rate or ratio (*e.g.,* one teacher to each twenty-five students).

The meaning of this, of course, depends first of all on how we counted teachers and students. To avoid argument with academics, we might better redefine our units as people who meet classes, and enrollees. Also we must remind ourselves that the real persons do not necessarily, if indeed ever, confront each other in the frequencies the ratio suggests. The ratio is merely a casual guess as to the most likely arrangement to expect by chance, and contrary to the opinion of some people, academic affairs rarely proceed entirely by chance.

One of the most useful modifications of the ratio is a statement of relationships in percentage or a ratio standardized to a base of one hundred. A minimum of four mathematical operations have been performed to obtain a percentage: two classes of events have been counted, the frequency of one has been divided into the frequency of the other, and the result multiplied by one hundred. Considered in this way, it is obvious that there is plenty of room for simple errors, but the simplest of all is the bland acceptance of the end figure as a kind of real object having a life of its own. In other words, people tend to treat percentages like match sticks, or houses, or dollar bills, rather than high-powered abstractions.

A parable: A teacher took a job as instructor at X college, and the second year he received a raise of ten per cent. The third year enrollment fell off, and the college was forced to cut everyone's salary ten per cent. "Oh well," he said philosophically, "easy come, easy go. I'm right back where I started." Not if he was a math teacher, he didn't! If this example trapped you, figure it out on paper with a starting salary for the instructor of, say $30,000, which is just as realistic as thinking that ten per cent equals ten per cent, if you have not first made certain that the two percentages are computed from the same, and reasonable, base. Even comparing figures as percentages of the same base is misleading if the base figure is not understandably related. As an example, compare your salary to that of the head coach at a university as percentages of (a) your son's weekly allowance, and (b) the national debt, and see which one, if either, makes you feel better. The sober, unhappy point is that both of these two kinds of errors are offered constantly in newspapers, journals, speeches, and elsewhere, and often the author blandly omits any definition of the base whatsoever, *viz:* "Things are looking better. Business volume is up ten per cent!"

Moral: 400 per cent is better in baseball than in taxes.

Our society has so often eulogized man's best friend that only the most obtuse statistician would conclude that a typical man-and-his-dog average three legs, but every day good, average people make errors just as gratuitous on the average in using averages. To speak of the average height of a group of men and women or the average age of the audience at a grade school play may yield results which, while less shocking, are fully as bizarre. Here again, as with most common statistical devices, few people really understand mathematically what the formulas mean, and yet they develop a kind of mystical feel for their use. "Average man" calls up an image of the man who lives across the alley. "Average day" means one distinguished from the rest neither by drama nor by excessive monotony. In fact, most people's approach to the whole business of averages is so intuitive that when the statistician writes "mean" they automatically translate it to "feel," because the mean is meaningless.

To be sure, the sophisticated have learned that average includes medians and modes, and many even know that for some reason salaries are better discussed in terms of the median (that coach is somehow involved in this again), but very few people have learned that there are times when you should not "take an average" at all. Most of us go ahead and take them on general principles, just like Grandpa took physic. Of course, when Grandpa had appendicitis, the physic killed him. You can't go against nature (or God) that way. But nature (or God) is less prompt in punishing statistical errors, with the result that many folks develop a real talent for sin.

Moral: How mean can you get?

Correlation is one of the handiest devices yet devised, and correspondingly, one of the least understood. Unless you have had a course in statistics, you probably do not know the formulas for this one, which may be just as well, considering how many people take means and how popular a catchword correlation has become. Most people think it is a high-powered word for cause. Actually it is not. In fact, "it" is not anything, because "it" is a "they." While correlation customarily refers to Pearsonian *r* (because this is an easy formula for people with easy consciences), there are numerous ways of computing correlations, each with subtly different meanings but all with one thing in common: correlations are simply mathematical statements about the degree to which some varying things tend (or don't tend) to vary together. A long time ago, John Stuart Mill painstakingly explained that even when causes were somehow involved, you could not safely infer that one of the variables in the correlation was causing the other; but Mill is out of fashion these days, and correlations are popular. Perhaps a good example of spurious causal reasoning might be the very high positive correlation between the number of arms and the number of legs in most human populations, which clearly proves what I have claimed all along, that arms cause legs.

There is no point in the math-fearing layman's even

trying to grasp when and how to use the various correlation formulas. You simply must study some mathematics to gain even a hint of the restrictions, because the restrictions grow in part out of the kind of data with which you deal and in part out of the mathematical assumptions you make in trying to get the job done. If the mathematical assumptions are not met reasonably well by the data (and they almost never are!), the resulting statement about relationships among the data is, in greater or lesser part, grounds for libel. But data, like nature and God, are slow to respond to statistical calumny; so let us only seek to protect the reader.

Two other forms of correlation are beginning to appear in public, with their own characteristic misinterpretations: these are multiple and partial correlation. If correlation means the mathematical relation between two sets of variables, then multiple correlation means relationships between three sets or more. Fair enough? This is especially handy when trying to describe a complex set of interactions, such as rush hour traffic, or the stock market, or many human behaviors in which opposing and cooperating forces are working, pushing, and shoving, not working in any clearcut simple direction, but nonetheless producing some kind of result. The "feel" most people have for correlation carries over into multiple correlation, with probably not much greater inaccuracy. Instead of feeling one thing affecting another, they can go on feeling several things affecting another.

The real fun comes with partials. Multiples are confusing "because of" (or correlated strongly with) the fact that they describe complex situations. Partials are confusing because with them we symbolically do what we can't do in actual practice (but would love to!): we simplify the situation by making everything hold still except the one thing we wish to examine.

"Now," says the layman, "you're getting somewhere. I *knew* there was a simple answer to all this if you would just produce it. What was that partial correlation for income and juvenile delinquency again?" Alas, we are worse off than before, because with multiple correlation we convinced him the problem was complicated (although not for exactly the reasons he supposed); but now we have inadvertently proven to him that it is all very simple, and that all effects may be understood in terms of simple, discrete causes. If I become inarticulate here, it is because in my town a layman (nice, average sort of man) published a statement in which he said income had virtually no relation to juvenile delinquency, and cheerfully cited a partial correlation to prove it.

What he did not know and I failed to explain to him was that partials rule out the joint effects of several variables *mathematically,* although these effects may be present and important *empirically*. For example (and here my analogies really strain their mathematical bonds!), in samples of water, the multiple correlation between hydrogen and oxygen and the phenomenon called wetness is high. The partial correlation for hydrogen and wetness, holding oxygen constant, is near zero. The same goes for the partial between oxygen and wetness, with hydrogen held constant. At this point I hope the readers bellow in a chorus, "You idiot, it takes both hydrogen and oxygen *together* to produce water!" Amen, and it probably takes low income, broken homes, blighted residential property, and a host of other things, all intricately intertwined, to produce juvenile delinquency. To say that the partial correlation with low income, all other factors held mathematically constant, is near zero, does not mean we can forget it in real life. It more probably means that this one factor is the constant companion of all the rest.

Clearer illustration of multiple and partial correlation

may be seen in the *State Fair* mince pie, to which each member of the family surreptitiously added brandy. Each did just a little, but the whole effect on the judge was a lulu. To attribute some portion of the binge to any single person's brandy contribution would have only symbolic meaning, and hardly would be identifiable empirically, but it could not be ruled out. Moral: Camels may ultimately collapse under straws.

Most teachers have been exposed to the Normal Curve, usually in the form of an edict from the administration concerning the proper distribution of grades to hand out. In fact, in one institution some misguided administrator computed the percentage distribution of grades for my class of six students and compared it to the proposed institutional curve. The curve is what you might expect to find if the frequencies of events ranged around some mid-point purely by chance, like the impact points of artillery shells fired as exactly as possible at a given target. The mathematical specifications of the curve are complicated, but the basic point to remember is that this is a curve of chance occurrences; in fact, some people call it the curve of error. If any factor, however small, consistently biases the possibilities of events, they will not group themselves in this sort of curve, and it is sheer tyranny for us to insist that they should do so. It is true that over a large number of cases (say ten thousand) of students taking a given test with a similar general background of ability and interest, the grades will *approximate* this sort of curve. But the principle on which the curve is predicted says explicitly in fine print that any given small portion (sample) of those ten thousand (universe) might pile up at either end, or in the middle, or might scatter all over it from here to Hoboken. This small sample is your class and mine, and it may not be just your imagination: it is perfectly possible, statistically, that they really are all F's this year! Another year they may be all A's.

Moral: The normal curve will never replace the *Esquire* calendar.

The theory of sampling is a beautiful and fearful thing to behold and none but the statistical priesthood should be trusted to gaze upon it. But the laiety should at least become pious and agree to some key points in the creed. First of all, size of sample is much (underline *much*) less important than almost everything else about the sample. A carefully designed sample of two hundred cases can tell more than a sloppily collected sample of two thousand. The basic problem in sampling is to get a sample which faithfully represents the whole population or universe from which it was drawn. All the elaborate machinery of sampling is set up to serve this purpose, and if the rules are not followed, the sample might as well not be drawn at all. Good sampling is neither cheap nor easy, while bad sampling is sometimes both. The casual layman who wants to know how to make a sample should be given the same advice as the man who asked a doctor at a dance what he would suggest in a hypothetical case of illness. You will recall that the M.D. said, "I would advise that man to see a doctor." The best advice before trying to draw a sample is to see your local statistician. Otherwise, don't do it yourself unless you are sure you know how.

Moral: A free sample may be good for a disease you don't have.

The question which must be answered about most information derived from sample surveys is: "Is this statistically significant?" What this means is: "Could the kind of frequencies of events we have discovered have occurred purely by chance?" On this kind of answer rests our confidence in the Salk vaccine, radar, strategy in sales campaigns, and many other kinds of events where the improvement or change we seek is not total but is nevertheless desirable. In some cases, as small a change as two or three per cent may be significant—that is to say, is not likely to have occurred merely by chance; while in others, a twenty or thirty per cent change may not be significant. The techniques of determining significance are a serious study in themselves, but the common sense cautions in using them may be summed up in two statements: a difference that does not make a difference is not a difference; and, there is a vast difference between statistical significance and importance.

KNOWLEDGE
WITHOUT NUMBERS

It would be nice if all of the data which sociologists require could be enumerated because then we could run them through IBM machines and draw charts as the economists do. However, not everything that can be counted counts, and not everything that counts can be counted. Often we must use nonquantitative methods, and there are really only two: you can get data by looking and drawing your own conclusions as to what you have seen; or you can get data from other people's verbal reports, oral or written, about what they think they have seen. Unfortunately the data are never any better than the people who see them. Whole books have been devoted to complaints about the strange ways in which human beings perceive, forget, and remember; but people are human and there is not much that can be done about it. If this disturbs you, perhaps you should quit sociology and take up white rats, viruses, or electrons.

Getting data of a sort is never a problem for the sociologist because his "data" are constantly all around him. His problem is to select so as to get just the signals he wants and screen out the noise. It follows that he must develop in advance some notion of the sorts of information he wants; in other words, his data-collecting is predetermined by his theory. This may sound like dirty pool; however, it is the way science always works, except in instances of serendipity, in which case you have the luck to find something you were not hunting and the good sense to apply it. Such brains and such luck are too infrequent to depend on in building a science. We have to plan our way or we don't go. But the planning or theory-making is complex in itself and we need not confuse it with research. Regardless of the kind and content of the guiding theory, similar research methods are used.

When we observe and communicate our information immediately, we call it reporting. Reports that come in late and cover more time are called history. Reports covering a long time about a particular, selected person or situation are called a case history; and if the time exhausts the life of the subject, it is called a life history. If the subject writes the report himself, it is an auto-biography. In each case, the basic process is that of a newspaperman who sees and tells. And we should remember that newspapers, histories, medical reports, and scientific accounts are all edited. At one time, social workers feared editing and tried to record everything that was said or done. This was called process recording. In a similar vein, Joyce and Proust wrote novels in which they tried to record everything that was said, done, and thought. Happily this day is past. We have realized that life is constantly being edited, whether intentionally or not, so we might as well accept editing as a responsibility and get on with it.

One way of editing is to restrict behavior in advance. When this is done well and systematically in the interest of science, we call it experimentation. Other people call it meddling. True experimentation is never a way of discovering anything but rather of checking to see if what we think we have discovered is true. When the doctor pokes you in one part of your body and says

"Does this hurt?" and then pokes you in another and asks "Does it hurt over here?" he is performing an experiment. At least two trials are necessary, the one to check on the other. Some people will say "yes" the first time as readily as they will the second. The reports of such people are not useful. Their answers do not discriminate. However, if the patient winces sharply when poked in his appendix and shrugs casually when poked in the left kidney, he helps the doctor test his guess, which in formal terms is called verifying an hypothesis.

An experiment essentially enables us to select between situations so as to confirm suspected cause-effect relationships. If we had a perfectly designed and controlled situation, we could run an experiment just once and be sure of the results ever after. We almost never have this, and most experiments are repeated many times with many subjects before the scientist is satisfied. Thus, in crude or refined form, statistics come to play a part in experimental method, and there is ultimately an imprecise blending of controlled observation and number magic.

All of the elaborate procedures in making controlled observations are intended to avoid an unintentional limitation of the results. We want to rule out any effects from unrecognized causes and thereby find out if what we think are causes actually do produce effects. This often takes a bit of doing, and in social science the costs are often prohibitive.

Even in the physiological sciences, crude approximations are often substituted. One of my friends in graduate school did his Ph.D. research on the nutrition of the mink. He personally loathed mink and would have preferred to study the nutrition of human beings, but he could get funds only to study mink. In Wisconsin, mink are a ten-million-dollar industry whereas people are not. Some folk are quick to say that you can't experiment with people because they won't stand for it, but this is only partly true. Mink are also notably uncooperative, but with enough money, time, and effort they can be studied. The basic limitation on sociological experiments is simply the lack of funds.

Our inability to select people to order and put them in controlled, standard situations to see how they react leads to substitutes. We can look for people who have just happened to undergo the experience which interests us and ask them what they observed about it. When we do this directly, it is called interviewing. Interviews which have been reduced to writing in a letter or postcard are called questionnaires. Interviews in which we attempt to find out more about the person than he realizes he knows are called depth interviews. In all cases, they involve someone else's report.

There are many tricks to the interviewing trade. Not every researcher can interview all people; in fact, most of us can only interview a rather narrow range, those who are somewhat like us. Moreover, some people are hard to interview, some are easy, and some are so easy you can't stop them. It also makes a difference whether you have to go to them or whether they come to you.

If the people you interview come to you voluntarily, the session may be formal or even brusque. This is what happens when someone applies for a job. The employer doesn't have to persuade the subject to be interviewed or cajole him into answering, and there is usually no more joviality than you might find in a magistrate's court. It takes no tact and not much intelligence to interview like this; you just take a list of questions, fire them at the subject, and put down his answers. It may, however, take a great deal of intelligence for someone else to figure out whether these answers are true. Some people defend this kind of interviewing (Kinsey was one) because they think the subject should be somehow badgered into telling the truth, as if he were afraid not to. I question this because, while some people might be frightened into telling the truth, I suspect that as many others may be frightened into concealing information, if not actually into lying. But both the proponents and the opponents of this method have a difficult case to make. We simply don't know.

The other extreme in interviewing is carried on by a participant observer. That is, someone who seems to be just another person in the situation and simply picks up his information as he finds it. This has the great potential advantage of getting information from people while they are off-guard, which means that you can learn things they would never reveal to a formal investigator. The disadvantages, however, are numerous. First of all, it takes time because you have to get the information when it is available, and this usually can't be predicted in advance. It also means that you must join their group; and should you wish to interview prostitutes, opiate addicts, or murderers, the difficulties are obvious. Not that it hasn't been tried. The criminologist Hans Riemer had himself sent to prison to get an inside look. But even though his crime and sentence were framed, he nevertheless had a record. Until the day he died, he always carried a sheaf of documents with him to explain to various officials that while he was an ex-convict, he wasn't really a criminal but rather a criminologist who had been a participant observer. It made a good story and one which most of the officials eventually enjoyed, but it consumed too much of his time. He did not recommend that anyone else try it.

Even in less extreme cases, participant observation presents another problem. If the interviewer collects his data too soon, he may get nothing more than an outsider could get because he hasn't had time to see things as the insiders do. On the other hand, if he waits too long, he may become so enmeshed in the group that he loses his objectivity and sees things as a loyal group member might. It is hard to be both insider and outsider at the same time, but this is what the job demands.

Add a further caution about participant observation. When you are successful and really get the inside information, publishing it makes you a traitor to the group. People invariably regard this as a kind of sociological badger game, a malicious *exposé;* and they may get quite surly about it. You call yourself a sociologist, but they call you a rat. If you want to sneak your interviews, you must not be disturbed when people call you a sneak.

This kind of interviewing is akin to eavesdropping, a field in which there have been many technological improvements in the last few years. Wire-taps which do not disturb the wires, pocket tape recorders, long distance microphones, and the like eliminate most of the practical problems, but raise a host of ethical ones. There is a fine line between doing research and peeping, and not long ago a couple of sociologists were widely accused of crossing the line when they secretly recorded the deliberations of juries. Their motive may have been good, but not their judgment nor their understanding of our society. They were fortunate that their technology was not too far ahead of public attitudes. As it was, the jurors were angry with them. A few years earlier, they might have been shot. If people keep information private, they have their reasons. A certain amount of judicious uncovering can be done, but it often takes very little prying to set off an explosion.

Information obtained in private should usually be kept private. A young social worker whom I knew was riding on a bus and chatting with a friend about a case she had. She had given no names but most of the interesting facts, when a stranger sitting behind her tapped her on the shoulder and said, "Excuse me, but that wasn't exactly the way it happened. . . ."

Most laymen have a mistaken notion that people won't tell intimate facts to strangers. Actually, they would often rather confide in a *bona fide* stranger who will have no way of using the information against them than a friend in whose hands it might be ammunition. Moreover, despite all our conventions about modesty, most people will more readily discuss their health or their sex life than their financial affairs. It is anyone's guess whether they lie more about sex or money.

A specialized kind of interview with a tightly formulated structure is a test. A test always involves a standard problem, directions about responding to it (which often include restrictions on time and method), and an arbitrary scoring system.

Since most people either do not wish to be tested or are psychologically disturbed and too eager to be tested, researchers have often tried to test people without their knowing it, or at least without their knowing exactly what is being studied. There are good reasons for doing this. We learned long ago that people who know they are taking a test act differently than they ordinarily would, similar to people who put on company manners for guests. This plays havoc with the data. As in the case of participant observation, you may have to sneak up on them.

The dissembling, or sneaky-type, test is called projective. The interviewer presents a situation such that the person he is studying projects, or puts his own feelings, biases, and desires into the result in such a way that the interviewer can spot them even though the subject doesn't know they are there. Psychoanalysts tell us that we project our own personalities into everything we say or do, so it is easy to devise projective situations. However, it is difficult to evaluate them; what is fact to one man is projection to another and the interviewer himself can easily over-interpret or project. Happily, only sophisticated subjects can deliberately mislead you because most people don't understand how projective tests work. In any projective technique you show or tell the subject something vague enough so that he can make his own sense of it. How he twists it and what he adds or subtracts provide your data. The most famous projective test is the Rorschach.

In most interview situations, the interviewer goes to the subject and must entice him to be interviewed. There must be something in it for the subject, although the something may vary. At one time, when surveys were novel, most people—at least most middle-class urban people—were flattered to be chosen. Rural folks are traditionally more suspicious, as are lower-class, urban people. Upper-class people can't be bothered or usually even reached.

The middle class also has changed. So many phoney advertising and sales campaigns have been built around a pretended survey that people are immediately suspicious. They usually ask what you are selling, which calls for credentials of some sort to prove that you are a legitimate researcher, a considerable amount of charm to hold them long enough to present your problem, and a convincing assurance that it won't take too much time or effort on their part. How you reassure them depends upon them; not all fish like the same bait. It also depends on what you appear to be, more than what you are. For many middle-class neighborhoods, the best interviewers are young college girls. They are clean, pretty, and polite, so that the householder probably will not slam the door on them as he might on a salesman. Of course, to send college girls into areas where robbery or rape is a threat is precarious. Here you may want a man, preferably a friendly, quiet, big man. A man who is big enough rarely has to prove his ability to defend himself, as policemen know. Even if they are not actually afraid, most people are rather eager to please a big dog. A big man draws a similar response.

Still different requirements may exist for interviews that you conduct in someone else's business office. One large book publisher used to have his salesmen appear with overcoat on the left arm, notebook in hand, and right hand extended as they strode in and introduced themselves. They would then pull up a chair while the prospective customer was still mumbling amenities. All of this took about four seconds, and was planned and executed as precisely as a military salute. The coat was a meaningful part of the act. It was supposed to say, "I am a busy man, and you are a busy man, so let's get down to business." The publisher seemed to think it worked, and certainly it gave his men an excuse to leave quickly and charge down the hall, while the more genteel approach favored by other firms took more time. Efficiency is probably the greatest merit of formal interviewing. If you can get the information you want just for the asking, you can print up a schedule of questions, sometimes even a schedule of possible answers, and tick them off one after the other. For some research, this will work, but not all. People may not tolerate the interruption, they may lie, they may refuse to answer at all. In short, they may slam the door.

In an informal interview usually material is expressed more fully, with less resistance, and probably less lying. But it takes time, and the material doesn't come in predictable order. If the interviewer doesn't exert any pressure at all, it is often incomplete. The ability to exert just enough pressure to elicit material without distorting it is the successful interviewer's art. A standard gambit is to tell a story of your own experience which deals with the kind of material you wish to get from the subject; he then feels obliged to respond in kind. If the interviewer is not careful, it can develop into a can-you-top-this session, but this approach usually gets response. Of course, it cannot be used on all people. Most folk will talk, however, and once they start, Carl Rogers' procedures help keep them talking. Basically, these amount to just rephrasing the speakers' last remark. "Oh, in other words . . . ?" This is usually enough to set them off again.

Another effective device is the hypothetical situation. It has endless variations, but basically the interviewer asks the subject something like: "Tell me, what would you do if a bear came down the chimney?" and then notes his reply. Closely related to this is the "Have you heard . . . ?" introduction. This one arouses suspicion, however, because it is another one which the salesmen have abused. A dead giveaway of the salesman is the cheery request for verification of a self-evident fact. This is often used in telephone pitches: "Mr. Cameron, I understand that you own your own home." Presumably, you are flattered that he knows your name and that he recognizes the dignity and honor that goes with having paid off the mortgage, or some part of it, and happily agree. But if you are familiar with what follows, you have a strong temptation, to which I nowadays always give in, to counter this with an equally impertinent question, such as "What makes you think so?" or "How did that information leak out?" or "What telephone number are you calling from?" or "Would you please give the name of your supervisor?" Anything will do; but the more upset you sound, the more you will upset him. After all, he called you, so you might as well get something out of this otherwise profitless encounter.

An additional abuse of the interviewing privilege which haunts legitimate investigators is the ruse employed by some sexually disturbed men who pretend to conduct an interview with women and girls concerning marital matters. It used to be that such characters identified themselves as psychologists, but apparently sociology has come of age because some now call themselves sociologists. When one of these incidents comes to the attention of a university, administrators are often reluctant to publish a denial, fearing that it might arouse more activity. There is no way to calculate the amount of ill will generated toward universities and research organizations in this way, but it is obviously considerable and makes the interviewing job that much more difficult.

Sales people and pseudo social scientists have so thoroughly discredited sample survey interviewing that it may take real skill to elicit even rather straightforward information. People are afraid that any reply may cost them something. Sometimes the false choice may make people answer. For example, some years ago one of my students was interviewing in a white, working-class area about racial integration. Most of the men he approached said either they didn't want to talk about it or they had no opinions. Too many of these "Don't know's" spoiled his sample so he applied some pressure. If someone turned him down, he would thank them pleasantly, close his notebook, and start to leave. Then he would turn back and say, "By the way, I'm curious about one thing. Are you not giving me any opinion because you haven't thought about this, or because you're afraid of what the neighbors will think?" Now, if you know working-class American males, you know that both of these alternatives are intolerable. Men do not want to admit that they have not thought about any public issue, and they certainly do not want to admit that they get pushed around. The typical retort was, "Hell, no, I don't care what the neighbors think. I think so-and-so!" After this opening, the student sometimes had trouble stopping them.

The problem of turning the subject off occurs mostly with people who are lonely and regard the interviewer as a new-found friend. In areas where ethnic etiquette demands that every guest should be fed, interviewing becomes both time-consuming and fattening. The first two or three interviews are fine, but after that it becomes difficult. The same goes for areas where people insist that you have a drink. Social workers encounter the same problem.

But all in all, interviewing can be fascinating work. It is full of surprises, most of them verbal. No interviewers I have known ever got into any real trouble, mostly because they were smart enough to know where not to go. But the demands of modern sampling techniques do not permit as much choice as they once did. This makes for greater precision in the survey but also more discomfort for the interviewer.

I recall Thomas C. McCormick regaling his class in research methods at the University of Wisconsin with reminiscences of his experiences with the federal government during the depression. "We had a map with all the counties in Arkansas on it, and we drew a sample of counties and then drew a sample of farmers from each county. This looked pretty simple in the office, but it was different when we got out into the field. Often we couldn't tell just exactly which county we were in. In fact, very often the farmer couldn't tell just which county he was in. And there were other things, too, which restricted the accuracy of the research. Along about noon, I noticed that we tended to select neatly painted houses with big barns, and we kind of shied away from the little old beat-up shacks, especially when there was a big dog in the yard." In methodological terminology, we might observe that putative culinary demonstrations exhibited a positive valence and large canines a negative valence in biasing the field-selection of respondents. But even without this kind of clarification, we got his point. A sample which can be chosen by the interviewer in the field will meet his personal needs better than those of the study.

Since most of the information obtained in an interview is expressed in language, it is obvious that choosing the right language is the most important problem at all times. This becomes critical when the interviewer and his subject are not from the same social background. Similar words can mean vastly different things, and often the mere use of a dissimilar word puts a chill on the interview. In a short interview which is carefully planned and edited by someone with a talent for translation, the confusing or alarming words can be chopped out. If the interview lasts longer, this is more difficult because the interviewer will have to *ad lib*. If the interviewer becomes a participant observer, there is no longer any risk; he will ultimately give himself away; the only question is "when?"

Some researchers think they can conceal their real identity, and for a time they may be able to do so. It is difficult to keep it up, though; and it may arouse suspicion when they are found out. For example, during World War II, I was sent as a replacement to a semi-literate army unit overseas and saw no profit in pointing up the fact that I had a master's degree, so I "passed." I had brought my command of military profanity to a high level of proficiency through infantry training, and I communicated fluently until I made friends and relaxed. Then, in a barracks argument, I inadvertently used a three-syllable word. I knew it was wrong the instant it came out and tried to pretend nothing had happened, but I knew the men were suspicious. A few days later one of my close friends told me, "Man, I had to explain you to those guys. They were real hostile, but I just told them 'Forget it. He doesn't mean anything by it. He's just had so much education he can't help talking that way!' "

Some interviewers try to duplicate the speech of the subject, but this is a dangerous practice. It helps, to be sure, if you can drop in a correctly used technical term here and there or sprinkle appropriate colloquialisms. But the trouble comes when you misuse one and don't know what you have said. Most people are aware that this can be done in a foreign language; they just don't realize how foreign are the sub-languages of the many regional, occupational, and ethnic groups in our own society. It is better to stick to basic English than to hack up the local jargon. A mistake in the local dialect will usually get you laughed at and sometimes get you shot. Even mentioning this possibility to an experienced researcher is a demand bid for the anecdotes which will follow. The obvious maxim is that all interviews in special groups should be conducted by your bright native guide.

I said that most of the information in an interview comes through language. It might seem at the outset that all of it does; but if this is true, the interviewer is incompetent. In the words of the old jazz record, "It ain't what you say, it's the way that you say it!" This reaches its peak perhaps in the psychiatric interview in which the psychiatrist pays attention to what you say, how you say it, how long it took you to get around to saying it, and what you carefully didn't say at all. Few of us will develop this degree of skill, but the principle holds. Even the timing of arrival may be a clue. An old adage among social workers goes: "If the client arrives early, he is anxious. If he arrives late, he shows resistance. If he arrives on time, he is compulsive!"

The important thing for the observer is to become aware of what various behavior *might* mean and then try to determine what it *does* mean. This is where the participant observer has the advantage, because in addition to what he learns from the casual kind of interviewing he does, he has lots of time and repeated opportunities to verify his hunches.

When you carry this sort of approach to its logical conclusion, you have the basic field method of the anthropologist, who has been defined as a sociologist who has lived among the Indians. Being a good field ethnologist takes an open mind and a strong stomach. The risk of going native, however, has been grossly exaggerated by the novelists. It takes a great deal more than an abstract love of your fellow man to enable you to live with him.

Whereas direct personal interviewing exposes you to stomach troubles or a possible sock on the jaw, sending out questionnaires exposes you to more evasion and deceit. Most studies based on mailed questionnaires are invalid from the start because so many people throw them away. You can hope that the people who answer do not differ appreciably from the people who refuse, but this demands careful testing. You also never know who is kidding you. Questionnaires often elicit wild answers. The trouble is, you don't know whether the tame ones or the wild ones are true.

Writing a good questionnaire is even harder than interviewing because a questionnaire must communicate at first reading. The respondent can't say "How's that again?"; moreover, he is disinclined to do so. If it does not make sense, he skips it, or just writes down anything to ease his conscience, or else he hands it to some underling to fill out for him. About the only virtue of questionnaires is that they are cheap, but in an economically oriented society this means that they are here to stay.

It is a lamentable peculiarity of sociologists that in their attempt to be objective they have lost sight of the main purpose of objectivity in the first place. We know that we should try to avoid letting our personal biases mislead us about the facts. To this end, we construct controlled experiments and other elaborate studies. But by the time we have diluted these to the level of the mailed questionnaire, we have largely lost what we set out to gain. If one sociologist makes a personal observation about an event, we call it a hypothesis, an opinion, or a guess. But if a thousand less intelligent and less interested people can be inveigled into filling out a return postcard, the tabulated total is regarded as research. Personally, I would rather trust the opinion of one bright trained observer than those of a thousand indifferent fools. Perhaps I have wandered into the camp of the anthropologist after all.

I started out talking about research without numbers, which is the way all research originally begins, but admittedly we would like to quantify where we can. The degree of sophistication in any science is about the same as the degree to which it can reliably quantify its data. Notice I said "reliably" because mere application of numbers is only confusing. In studies using discrete data, you can count, as long as you can identify what you count. This is easy with fence posts but hard with people because people don't stand still. All enumeration of people is approximate, and many times it is merely indicative. A measure which indicates is called an index. The construction of indices is a challenging problem and one in which considerable ingenuity can save considerable cash. In designing the census tracts for

Peoria, Illinois, we faced the problem of guessing population in newly built subdivisions for which we had no figures whatsoever. We worked up a crude estimate by driving through the area and counting the number of children's vehicles around each house—bicycles, tricycles, and the like. If we saw a house that appeared to have three bedrooms and outside it were two bicycles and a kiddy car, we guessed that five people lived there. (These were middle-class suburbs where we could assume that boys and girls occupy separate bedrooms and demand separate bicycles.) There are, of course, better ways to measure population, but we could not find better ways that were cheaper. In this sort of game, anyone with enough money can do it right, but it takes a clever researcher to do it nearly right for next to nothing.

Just as the experimental approach has blended with statistics, so also have some of the less rigidly controlled forms of observation. A number of statisticians have shown sympathy for sociologists to the extent of developing statistics which do not demand many assumptions about the data. These non-parametric statistics, as they are called, and the development of index numbers, even such as our bicycle-guess, are procedures which hold promise for future sociological work. They are not as good as we want, but they may be as good as we can get. Instead of knowledge without numbers, we will wind up with knowledge without many numbers, or a quasi-quantitative science.

There are endless minor variations on these few major themes, and most researchers would like to think that they have invented some new procedure which is better than that of anyone else. Their innovations sometimes excite a brief fad and then are seen as just another chorus on the same old chords. When we compare our research methods with those of the physicists and chemists, we have to say in all humility, "An ill-favored thing, Sir, but mine own." The only consolation is that when physicists and chemists try to carry their own skills over into the problems we deal with, they look even worse than we do. Numbers or not, test tubes or not, people are difficult to study.

REFLECTIONS
ON SOME ILLUSIONS*

About twenty-five years ago, sociologists in America began to take an active interest in a European importation called Sociology of Knowledge. The questions in this field seemed to center around the relations between the knower, the knowable, and the known. Perhaps the simplest way to express their central concern would be, "How do certain ideas come to be held by a particular group of people?"

From the start, the charge was made from various quarters that the only new answers sociologists were contributing to this question were a new name and a new vocabulary. Philosophers said that they had long studied the knowable under the heading of epistemology. Historians said that a number of the saints in this "new church" were really historians, and that the answers to the basic question were available once you had the historical facts about the people in question. Some scientifically biased sociologists replied to this that the historians could kid themselves into thinking *post hoc* meant *propter hoc* only because they never tried to predict anything, but the *true* social scientists were not only going to explain why people believed what in the past but also predict what who would believe in the

* Part of a paper delivered at the Midwest Sociological Society meetings, April 1959, Lincoln, Nebraska.

future. Amid cheers from young sociologists of the time could be heard dark muttering by older ones who had fought in the lists of methodology and wondered just what tactics would be used to produce the promised predictions. Nearby, psychologists smiled indulgently and said, "My dear fellows, have you just now discovered that man is not rational? We knew this all along!"

In retrospect, it now appears that several of these criticisms were true. The basic discovery of the field was, in a sense, the irrationality of man. No good student of history could be surprised by this, nor any psychologist who had read Freud, nor any economist who had read Marx, nor for that matter any theologian who had read Kierkegaard, although few had at that time.

It must also be admitted that sociologists from August Comte onward have taken too literally the statement that "in the beginning was the word." Before I knew enough about sociology to understand what he meant, the philosopher Elijah Jordan pointed out to me that one of the basic failings of sociologists was that they placed undue emphasis on the particular language with which their notions were expressed. Call it jargon trading, call it gobbledygook, the allegation is unhappily true, and many a good sociologist has deplored it. One wryly observed: "Words are like tooth brushes: we don't want someone else's in our mouths!" Another put it this way: "If you think you have an idea, unless you can put it in words the average intelligent layman can understand and give two or three quick examples, you don't have an idea." Much of the sociology of knowledge could not easily be translated for laymen.

Lest we offend anyone who is still strongly identified with the sociology of knowledge, let me hasten to point out that this is merely an example chosen to point up a difficulty which has long beset sociology, a kind of occupational disease which I think we should try to cure. The problem as I see it lies not directly with the sociology of knowledge, although this is an example, but rather is part of a more widespread problem, which inheres in the sociologist's manner of specialization.

Some academic disciplines have crammed so many concepts and methods under one heading that their name has become nearly meaningless. Psychology has done this. So many things are called psychology, and so many people with diverse interests and activities call themselves psychologists that the word tells you almost nothing about any of them. The content of even introductory texts in this field runs a gamut from physiology to salesmanship to several branches of philosophy, and many texts include as fundamentals materials totally alien to others. Sociology tends to go the other way.

Instead of just calling ourselves sociologists and saying that what we study is sociology, we tend to overspecify and treat as separate fields of study things which are at best concepts, or orientations, or in some cases only names of ideas which we hope to develop. Such a word as "knowledge" stands for a concept, and by the simple magic of combining it with "sociology of" we convince ourselves, and possibly others, that we have a new specialty. Most sociologists, like most physicians, long to be specialists. It reduces what you have to know, avoids embarrassing questions, limits competition, and in general protects prestige.

The result is that periodically we display a whole galaxy of glittering new areas of sociology. Currently we include sociology of art, sociology of education, sociology of law, sociology of religion, and so on, seemingly *ad infinitum*. All we need to do, it would seem, is to select some portion of culture, do a small study or two, and announce that there is a new specialty and people flock to identify themselves with it. This could easily be done in physics, if physicists wanted to do so. They could have the physics of houses, the physics of sports, the physics of crime, the physics of the kitchen, and so on, but they have been much less inclined to do so. The major areas of physics have for the most part been named and accepted only after there was a sufficiently large body of knowledge to make it economical to refer to it under some general heading, whereas in sociology we tend to establish the name and then try to develop the content. It is debatable whether greater specificity and complexity of our data demand this approach.

Along with the diversification of "areas" we have our gardens of special theories, unusually lush in social psychology. We have role theory, stratification theory, reference group theory, and others. As a young graduate student, I was impressed for a while with "field theory." That is, I was impressed until I tried to do something with it. I now like to call these "concept theories," because it seems to me that every time someone devises a useful or even nice sounding concept such as role, stratification, or reference group, it is immediately elevated to a theory. A true theory seeks abstractly to explain general processes which may be seen operating in a host of concrete detailed events and usually is the result of much speculation and many testings in many different situations. Most of these concept theories are merely cases of details wagging dogma.

Although I have digressed at length from the sociology of knowledge, I think it was necessary to put the main problem in perspective. The point is that the problems which afflict one branch of sociology and infect its theories are found throughout sociology as a whole and local surgery will not help, although some form of general radiation treatment might.

To return to the story of the sociology of knowledge, the dark forebodings of the older sociologists were indeed prophetic. At the point where sociologists of knowledge tried to predict, they unearthed all the old methodological problems, and on questions pertaining to research methodology sociologists traditionally have split into two main groups: the "understanders" who believe in artistic, insightful, and talented *verstehen* (intuitive understanding which goes beyond demonstrable data); and the "operationalists," (or perhaps we could call them the operators) who demand objective measurement, statistical manipulation, and Latin square experimental designs. Each of these fraternities has called the other dirty names. The "hard scientists" in the operational group deplore the studies of literature as mere novel-gazing, and in general regard the "verstehers" as dilletantes or mystics. The "softer" but perhaps more understanding scientists have called the painstaking researches of the rigidly empirical sort fireplug-counting (or worse!) and complain that the things the operationalists go around counting are unimportant.

Happily the reflections that characterized the search for a sociological theory of knowledge help to illuminate this internecine controversy. Although the sociologist may not be able to heal himself, he can at least diagnose. It boils down to this: there is a difference between proving something and being convinced. The special concern in the sociology of knowledge is to describe the grounds and processes of conviction, whereas most of the methodological work in sociology has dealt with proofs. From what we have learned, the old statement that "a man convinced against his will is of the same opinion still" might be rewritten to read: "a man who has seen a proposition proved which contradicts his sentiments is not convinced at all." Not as poetic, but it describes an important feature of most ideological struggles.

Proof means that we have submitted an idea to some kind of decision-making machinery, such as a truth table, a spectroscope, or a piece of litmus paper. Conviction sometimes follows, often precedes, and not infrequently continues despite proof.

One of the characteristics which distinguishes man from other animals is his ability to form opinions. Both man and beast react, but man alone opines. Moreover man prides himself that his behavior is guided by his carefully wrought opinions, and he stubbornly demands to see proof or to see the facts. But a careful look shows immediately that man's opinions are not formed *by* facts and proofs but rather *in response to* them. Since psychoanalysis and the sociology of knowledge overturned rational man, social scientists have been somewhat sadder, a little wiser, and considerably less self-confident about the intellectual integrity of man.

In any situation where man cares enough about the outcome to pay attention to what is going on, he usually cherishes some notions about how it *should* turn out. These may or may not coincide with his expressed guess about how it *will* turn out. Some folk are professionally optimists and others pessimists. Boxers traditionally predict success and football coaches failure. Even scientists are rarely objective about consequences; when they are, it is an objectivity of procedure and not the flattened affect of disinterest. A scientist is one who has learned how to take his medicine from reality.

Although we sociologists call ourselves social *scientists,* we also exhibit the curious ways in which conviction and proof are related. Examine *our* introductory textbooks. We used to cite the stories of feral men to prove that the human personality is of bio-social origin.

The stories were not well verified, but they sounded so good. Currently we lean more on Sherif's experiment with the auto-kinetic effect, in which it was shown that people could be influenced by others to perceive something that was not there, and that the norms of perception established in the group persisted even when the individuals dispersed. This is a very famous experiment. In our field, a man only needs to do one neat experiment to become famous, if that experiment accords with our convictions.

The fact is that despite the advances of science and philosophy, most of the important decisions in the world are made on only partially systematic grounds. Love, war, and the stock market all employ *verstehen*. To be sure, scientists must try to reduce *verstehen* to a book of formulas, but as the man said about his fat wife, why despise what we can't reduce? Economics is no doubt the most tightly developed social science, but an economist friend of mine often says that if all the economists in the country were laid end to end they still would not reach a conclusion.

While we are noting vagaries in sociology, let no one try to squirm out of his responsibility to think for our discipline by showing us the recent "game theory." Although it has had a slight vogue, as generally presented it is such an oversimplified analogy of human behavior as to amount to little more than a shabby mathematical pun. It is a pleasant enough game, but hardly a theory of human behavior.

When the psychoanalysts and social anthropologists discovered each other in the mid-1930's, they started another fad. The anthropologists needed a theory of personality and the psychoanalyst had grown philosophically nearsighted from staring so long at the couch. For a brief period, these Neo-Freudians seemed to have the answer. But they, too, often over-generalized. After

World War II, a psychiatrist who had just returned from Okinawa thought that breastfeeding had permanently protected the Okinawans from social disorganization and neurosis. He ought to see them today.

Recently there has been a rage for studies of small groups, handsomely supported by the Air Force and other large foundations. This is the microcosm for some people, who expect to see the solutions of large social conflicts presented in miniature behind a one-way vision screen and preserved by an interaction recorder. Richard Dewey summarized a sociologist's relation to this when he likened it to a man looking under a lamp post for a nickel he had lost down the alley. Under the lamp post there is more light!

Apparently, when new and potentially valuable ways of looking at problems originate, their adherents are blinded to traditional difficulties and confused by the new terminologies they help create, so that a hiatus temporarily develops between the new specialties and the old body of knowledge. After a time, translations are effected so that the new areas can be seen in relation to the old, and often we discover that what we had thought, or at least hoped, would be a vital new discovery is largely a rediscovery of ideas expressed earlier by Simmel, Cooley, Durkheim, and others whom we cease reading once we pass our doctoral examinations. The research findings of the new specialties may be valuable, but the confusion in communication which too often accompanies them is not.

Young sociologists should be warned that the problems in our field are demons which can hide and reappear at will, wearing different disguises and answering to new names. Collective behavior has had several names but we still study it. Country folk differ from city folk in interesting ways, be they sacred, simple, primitive, mechanical, or what-have-you. As Luther Bernard and

Charles Josey proved, attacking a name like "instinct" merely scotches the snake; the idea persists under different designations.

The sociology of knowledge is not and never was really different from the sociology of art, or the sociology of education, or any of the rest. There was no truly independent body of theory in these areas nor did there need to be. There are only a few basic concepts in each discipline, and excessive efforts to pile up others gains little in the long run and wastes much energy. In our field the most basic concepts are person, group, and culture. All of our basic problems and all of our useful knowledge deals with relations among these. When you describe how a biological individual living in a group learns to participate in a culture you are being a sociologist, whether you call yourself a social psychologist or an anthropologist, whether you say you are studying acculturation, or stratification, or social mobility, or the sociology of knowledge.

As sociologists our job is to describe real human behavior, and we only deceive ourselves if we think our major job is to rotate statistical matrices, or collect artifacts, or construct artificial human groups. Furthermore, after all of our most scientific work is done, any practical use of our findings will have to employ some *verstehen,* whether we enjoy it or not. A very great deal of what we think we know may always remain plausible and not provable. We may always have to depend upon insight, and so far there is no dependable method of providing insights apart from waiting for wise and talented people to get them. The proponents of several of these earlier specialties hoped to give us such a method, but we can see now that what they offered was not a compact and self-contained tool like the physicist's oscilloscope, but rather an orientation, a point of view, an interest in a set of problems. The old problems are as real as ever. It is to these problems that we must still address our efforts, and not to their various and confusing names.

In our daily work as sociologists we need to keep the following in mind:

Sociology is a single discipline. Pretentious specialization leads us away from basic problems into the haggling defense of special positions, reduces communication in an area where communication is always difficult, and diverts energy into wasted efforts. Instead of worrying about our specialty and how it rates, and whether we carry the name with the greatest prestige, we should pay more attention to the basic problems in the field.

There is no royal road to theory. There are no quick, easy schemes which are worth having or which are likely to last beyond the publication of the original prolegomena. Some sociologists long to devise a grand strategy which others will adopt and follow out. They want to found schools. They try to stake claims which will pay dividends later in the form of citations in footnotes or reprintings in anthologies. This is demeaning and, furthermore, often it does not even work. The other man may be too busy trying to sell his own grand plan to read ours.

There are no quick, practical solutions and we should not promise them, even by implication. We can occasionally say something useful to the man of affairs, but our model should be that of the scholar and the scientist not the commercially employed engineer. We should only reluctantly add the troubles of the legislature and the marketplace to those which already exist in library, the laboratory, and the classroom. When we are really sure of our theories there will be time enough to apply them. Meanwhile, it is far better to keep chipping away at basic problems than to try to peddle solutions. Solutions are a dime a dozen; get yourself a set of good problems and they will last you a lifetime.

Simple statements are often useful. At least you stand some chance of figuring out what they mean and whether they are right. Conceptual formulations which are pretentiously elaborate can make even a pretty good idea look ridiculous, but on the other hand, a good theory can easily survive statement in simple words.

ALL THE KING'S HORSES

Social science at one time built its case around the Great Man theory whereby the important social phenomena of any given time and space were explained by describing and analyzing some dominating individual whose personal characteristics directed the activities of other men and shaped their social world. This theory accompanied the rise of individualism of various sorts and was enthusiastically embraced by many social scientists and especially by historians at a time when the general populace still followed the older Great God theory.

As you might expect, if you have examined the course of history with an eye upon the way cultural traits diffuse, after a period of lag, this theory, propounded by energetic and prestige-laden men, and serving well as a rationale for activities already begun, succeeded to the throne of common reason. It is true that some peacemakers tried to devise for it an honored and divine lineage (as when the historian J. H. Breasted invested Akhnaton with divine inspiration), but most said, in effect, *The King is dead. Long live the King.* In an age of robust adventures—geographical, commercial, and ideational—Man supplanted God as a principle of explanation.

This sort of basic principle is generally accepted by the layman today who finds the course of recent history bound up in the names he reads in the headlines: Khrushchev, Kennedy, Nehru, DeGaulle, Mao.

Of course most social scientists now know the Great Man theory to be inadequate, at best. Most scientists, and many laymen, too, now "know" that the Great Man theory is false and await with tolerance or hasten with propaganda its early demise. But we might question whether greater truth will be found in denying it than was found in asserting it. In fact, we are now witnessing the ascent of a genuine counterpart to the Great God and the Great Man theories—the theory of the Great Culture.

No one individual need be given credit for originating this view. It would be inconsistent with the theory itself to credit it to any one man, a point which is made explicit by two of the most lucid exponents of this approach, Leslie White and Elijah Jordan.* If we may accept White's version of the theory as explanation of its origin, this theory is the natural culmination of many experiences which many men have had, and were it not White or Jordon, it would soon be someone else who would formulate it, in somewhat different language and with minor changes in form, but with equivalent effect.

In White's words, culture has a life of its own. In Jordan's, things have will. This does not mean, as it might seem to at first that these men impute some kind of animistic psyche to machines. Nor do they see man himself as a Frankenstein or a Pygmalion. But they have both, in separate ways, seen through the romantic notion of free will, both in its barroom, chest-beating, Hemingway approach and in the pseudo-scientific cant of Spencer's doctrines of evolution, and they have reduced the notion of will to what can be observed

* See *Selected Readings* at the end of this book for representative works by these men.

about it. In a very real sense, these men are behaviorists, and look at behavior as behavior, even when the behavior is the grudging reluctance to move which characterizes a heavy stone. At least one of Jordan's phrases, "the coerciveness of corporate structure," is widely accepted today. It is clear to most modern men that the business corporation is something more than the men who make it up and that it leads its leaders. But this is only an aspect which many men understand dimly, if at all, simply because they have batted their heads repeatedly against it. If we follow this line of thought consistently, we see that the entire culture is coercive, and that civilization, like the corporation, has a life of its own.

Recently novelists have produced a number of fictionalized accounts of the way man is coerced by the commercial sub-culture, especially in its Madison Avenue forms. Such descriptions, which use grey flannel suits, executives suites in which furniture denotes status, and gold plated keys to the executive washrooms as symbols, present in popular, fictional form ideas which only a few serious thinkers held some forty years ago: namely, that the business runs the man more often than the man runs the business. This may be common parlance today, but it was a discovery a generation or so ago.

There is always a temptation to see history as unfolding in a single line, even when we are looking at the history of ideas. There is continuity, but diversity is nearly as much the rule. Yet we have a great deal of similarity and continuity to explain. Sometimes we explain this away by pointing out the independent invention of ideas; and many ideas are arrived at independently and nearly simultaneously by various men. But on the other hand, if we take continuity and similarity as the model of the history of man's thought, we must then explain a continuing wide diversity. Even in this age, some men insist on a Great God theory and trace all events to the hand of deity. Happily for them, inconsistency on the part of God is already accounted for: "The Lord moves in mysterious ways his wonders to perform." However, a revived enthusiasm for theological explanation may be what John Dewey and Sidney Hook decried as "the new failure of nerve." It has always been difficult to distinguish the awe which is reverence from the awe which is plain fear, and man has much to fear.

At election time, most of us behave as if we still held to the Great Man theory, and we vicariously revel or despair, depending upon the success of our champion. (In a democracy you can't tell a David from a Goliath without an election.) We need to feel that our hero can solve all the problems which we dimly perceive and profoundly fear. A critical look at recent political leaders must make us doubt that any of them is an Oedipus, or for that matter that all us Thebans together can solve the riddle which the atomic age Sphinx has posed.

In many of the classical paradoxes, it can be shown that the confusion lay in treating things which were several in nature and usage as if they were one. This seems to be the case here. The Great God theory, the Great Man theory, and the Great Culture theory, each persuasive within its bounds, apprehend different questions. So long as men continue to address themselves to different questions, even though they do so only implicitly, they may be expected to adopt different theories. But this sort of observation, basic though it may be, is of little practical use to us unless we can delineate the areas wherein each such theory may profitably be applied. When new continents are first explored, many and various maps are drawn, all of which must later be corrected in the light of more adequate knowledge.

That knowledge itself is derived in part from the use of these poor maps. Science involves the art of making maps or guides.

In assuming the name of scientists, we must humbly lay aside the Great God theory, because in the nature of things, we limit ourselves to those incomplete and partial data which our senses may give us, assisted from time to time by various tools which we can devise. There can be no science of God, for by definition He is above science and scientists. This is a long way from saying we must become atheists, because atheism demands as uncritical a faith as most theologies and is usually less graceful in the bargain. It seems that scientists can not get very far working in this direction. There has been fine scholarship in theology and capable men still work in this area, but they are not and cannot be scientists, and nothing is gained by either theologians or scientists deceiving themselves about this.

Most of the time we do not concern ourselves directly with the behavior of God, or the Culture, or Great Men anyway, except as interested bystanders. Our more constant concern is with the behavior of smaller segments of culture and with the behavior of lesser men with whom we must interact every day. Some fundamental questions from this point of view are how a man comes to be a social animal at all, and how he may direct the process with his children. Stated more generally, what are the sources and limitations of individual human behavior? How may the behavior of individuals be integrated with that of others to form a society?

It is with these questions and others which can be derived from them that sociology is basically concerned, and along with sociology are allied on the one hand psychology, and on the other economics, political science, and law. It is true, of course, that few men in any of these fields work directly at these basic problems, but if man's outward behavior is shaped by his institutions, which are abstract and can care nothing for his hopes and fears, his thought is directed by such basic problems, whether he recognizes them or not. And in the long view of history, there are only a few such basic problems which continue and recur.

Man is an imperfectly social animal, and one of his recurring problems is the problem of freedom and order. It is restated from time to time, and in some periods we focus on freedom and in others on order, but the problems are inseparable, and no perfect solution has ever been found. Most men think about these things only when external situations force them to do so. Even great men think only when driven by demons, and the finest works on political and economic order have been written in times of actual political and economic chaos, from Plato to the present. Man is still too much of an animal to bother thinking hard about order in those periods in which a relatively stable society can be taken for granted.

While the question of freedom is an interesting one, science has never been able to say much about it. In fact, for a scientist, freedom is always a residual category: that is, freedom is what gets left over after he has described everything he can understand; or else freedom is the convenient category into which he can lump all the events which take place before the phenomenon he is interested in appears. It is somewhat like the chaos which existed before Chronos, because for the most part, science proceeds chronologically, noting what events precede and what events follow, and trying to map out sequences which will recur.

Science is concerned with the description of order, and especially chronological order, so that we can say, "If A occurs, then B will follow." While some of science is pure description of the parts and patterns of static objects, the more interesting part is the description of processes, or the ways in which orderly change takes place. This concept of process combines the idea of order and the idea of change.

What this means in practice is that we arbitrarily choose some starting point and tell what happens from here. Our starting point is never really the beginning of anything. In fact, some theories deny the whole notion of beginning. Most scientists in practice shrug off the question of beginning and the question of end as well and rather try to plot what is happening during a given time. They leave beginnings and ends to theologians and philosophers. When this fact about science is clearly recognized, it disturbs most people, because they are used to organizing their thought in terms of goals and purposes and they try to see events as milestones along a road. It bothers them to think that anyone could systematically ignore the question of where the road is going. Indeed, after the development of the atom bomb, this sort of question suddenly bothered a great many physicists, who had previously managed to ignore it. The fact that the development of knowledge is not like a well planned trip along a highway, plus the ability of some men's minds to sail blissfully over mountains which other men feel obliged to tunnel through, helps to account for the great variety of theories about human behavior. Some of these theories take as data things which others regard as pure speculation. All theories must start with assumptions, but often the assumptions are unclear, even to the founders of the theories. However, at this point, some of these routes of thought have been travelled so often by so many different men that if they are not highways, at least they are well worn ruts and we can map them with relative ease.

If we look beyond the Great theories at the range of

explanations which scientists have offered to account
for human behavior, we find that they can be grouped
into four main classes. All of these are deterministic, as
it was once held that all scientific theories must be. The
four can be called: organic determinism, situational determinism, cultural determinism, and individualism.

The earliest scientific theories about human behavior
tended to be organic, and this was in part due to the
successes of chemists and biologists whose concepts
and methods were borrowed wholesale. A number of
organic determinisms still persist today. The instinct
theory attempted to explain behavior essentially by
classifying the properties of various species of animals
and saying, in effect, "If this is a man then he will behave in this way." This theory came in for a lot of harsh
criticism, but many people today still use this kind of
a theory, with indifferent success. Whereas the instinct
theory sought to explain the behavior of an entire species, narrower versions of organic determinism have
been applied to races, to the separate sexes, or to different body types. There are observable differences in behavior which at one time or another may accompany
racial differences, and men do behave in ways in which
women do not.

The trouble with most racial or sexual theories is that
they stop where they should begin. The differences are
data and should be explained. Merely asserting that
men behave differently than women because they are
men may allow some degree of prediction, but it ex-
plains nothing. When the question of body types is
examined, some of the discussions become more sophisticated and try to relate subtle differences in reaction
time, body chemistry, and other physiological variables
to outward anatomical differences. At the layman's
level however, this still remains pretty crude, on a par
with Shakespeare's "Yon Cassius hath a lean and

hungry look." Even some professionals think like this. A pediatrician once told me that my six-month-old daughter was a pyknic type and proceeded to tell what personality characteristics to expect. He would be annoyed, perhaps, to learn that at age ten she had become asthenic instead. Obviously the body is part of the personality, but the connections between the persistent anatomy and the variable behavior are not as simple as such theorists wish.

Situational determinism attempts to explain behavior by its context, without regard for the biological character. As with other points of view, this one comes in both vulgar and refined types. The vulgar situational determinism can be seen in the frequent assertion that every man has his price. The refined version was developed by the psychological school called behaviorism, as represented by John Watson. He did not believe naively that the immediate situation was the entire answer, but he assumed that repeated exposure to specific situations molded the personality in precisely predictable ways. Doctors, lawyers, and Indian chiefs could all be made to order through the magic of conditioning.

Cultural determinisms can be roughly subdivided into philosophical, anthropological, and ethnocentric types. Hegel is a good example of the philosophical. He believed that culture was something above and apart from mere individual men, and that it was presided over by a World Spirit which determined its content and ultimately its success in competition with other cultures. Men were a kind of by-product of this all important culture. This view is of course too mystical for immediate scientific application, but Hegel's ideas influenced a great many social scientists, especially on the continent, and they came up with more modestly stated versions of it, which in the long run were no better. This kind of thinking was also perverted into Nazism by Hitler's friends.

Most anthropologists hold a more respectable form of cultural detemininsm. Since they know how differently men behave in different cultures, and since it is obvious that children learn what their elders can teach, it is an easy step to assert that man is what his culture makes him. For non-anthropologists, this often seems like the cart before the horse, because culture is itself man-made. The complication here is that no one man makes much new culture; he learns more than he invents, and we have a question much like the paradox of the chicken and the egg.

The ethnocentric view is often a vulgar one, which asserts that our ways of doing things are the best and every other society is backward. This is one of the oldest ideas in the world, and in the languages of many people the word for "Man" is the same word which they call their own tribe. We are not quite so simple, but we still regard all others as doubtful equals when the chips are down.

Individualism can be voluntaristic, rationalistic, or romantic, and probably other things as well. An example of voluntarism is the old notion of free will. I am what I choose to be. This idea appeals to us from the moment when, as small children, we first learn to say: "No!" While it is dressed up from time to time in fancy garb and surrounded with the trappings of various kinds of mysticism, it never really develops much from this negative position. It is man asserting that the world doesn't faze him. He usually protests too much.

The rationalistic view of individualism is quite involved, and some elaborate and subtle philosophies have been constructed along this line. Descartes is the usual prototype, but there are many others. Existentialism adopts this notion, along with pessimisms of various sorts.

Romantic individualism is the most common type, and this is generally pleasant and often exhilarating. For sheer unfettered exercise of the imagination, this view has few equals. See any issue of *True* magazine for happy examples. Give any man a gun and a wilderness and he feels like Daniel Boone, at least until he gets himself treed by a bear. Much literature, some of it technically good, proceeds from this point of view, and it may be fair to admit that a little romanticism is good for us all, so long as we are not carried away into believing the fantasies about ourselves which we so joyously create.

Each of these major points of view has some merit, and can marshall some evidence in its own behalf. Also, each of them is antagonistic in some way to the others. Organic determinism denies that the situation can change the result. To admit this undermines its own case. People's personalities, that is to say their behavior, ought to stay put so that we can predict. Situational determinisms, on the contrary, deny both the organic limitations of individual men and also fail to allow for the way in which apparently similar situations may differ in another cultural setting. A European psychologist admitted that he had to relearn how to use the Rorschach test when he came to this country. The standard ink blots simply did not present the same situation in Europe and in America. Not all situations change from culture to culture, but you can't be sure in advance which ones do.

We have already noted some obvious weaknesses in cultural determinism, and basically they stem from the denial of individual differences. Every culture loses some of its members through crime, mental disorder, and self-destruction. It is questionable whether they all lose the same kind. Man is not completely adaptable to culture, and some men may adapt more readily to one than to another. The individual is not merely a machine for maintaining cultural continuity. As for individualism, this notion is a surprisingly sturdy one, because it persists despite a severe daily beating from the complex social structures which press in upon us. Perhaps this is why young people hold this notion more strongly than old people. Old people have felt too many bruises.

In brief, each of these views is plausible and none is completely true. We can see now that a satisfactory explanation of human behavior must include knowledge of the species, the biological individual, the society, the culture, the immediate social group, the physical situation, the state of the individual's will, and the history of his previous reactions. This is too large a list of parameters to try to assemble into a formula, and it is for precisely this reason that there is as yet no Ohm's Law for human nature.

Let me now add one final cautionary note concerning some pitfalls in the road to theory-making of any sort, and especially to theories of human behavior. The two major hazards are tautology and reification. They can entrap any theory which man can devise and have done so in various fields of study. The history of the instinct theory provides an instructive example. In simple terms, tautology means reasoning in a circle; reification means making a thing out of something which is not a thing, or in other words, attributing active vital force to something which is actually only a construction of our own imagination, an abstract concept. Let us look at our example.

The instinct theorists observed what men did. They found that some actions were frequently, even almost continuously, repeated. Take, for instance, fighting.

With mathematical notation we can say that they observed $fighting_1$, $fighting_2$, $fighting_3$, and so on to $fighting_n$. They summarized this by collecting these observations under the heading of *The fighting instinct*. So far, they are safe. But when faced with a new instance of fighting, which we could call $fighting_{n+1}$, and obliged to explain it, they said it was "because of the instinct to fight." Now at this point they had made two large jumps. First of all, they had generalized their previous observations into a fighting instinct, and then they had endowed this abstraction of their own making with the force to cause another event of the same sort, or if we wish to be reflective, to cause all of the previous events of the same class. The instinct never caused anything, because the instinct was just a name men had applied to a collection of data. Explaining the data by its collective self is the same kind of reasoning employed by the man who said "I'm glad I don't like spinach, because if I liked it I'd eat it, and I hate the stuff!"

This error is not confined to the work of some earlier psychologists. The same reification and tautology are seen every day as, for example, when people say that gravity is what keeps us on the earth. You could just as well say that motion makes the world go around. To be sure, you are fairly safe in predicting that men will continue to fight, and that we will continue to be attracted to the earth, and that it will continue to go around. At least we have no good evidence to make us doubt these crude predictions, but predictions of this sort are not explanations. In fact, such predictions are apparently successful because they are so general that they preclude any real testing, since they do not admit conditions under which they might fail.

We are forced to conclude that theory making is a difficult task but an essential one. Since man can remember the past and imagine the future he needs theories almost as much as he needs shelter and food. The more intelligent man is, the greater are his theoretical needs. Moreover, the more he knows about the world and the people in it, the more he despairs of ever really understanding it. More than anything else, it is this intellectual despair which probably attracts him to one or another form of theology and religion. Since he tries to see himself as rational and the world as ultimately reasonable, and since his reason eventually leads him to the conclusion that he cannot understand the world, he must feel that to the Deity at least it all makes sense.

PHYSICAL SETTING AND INTELLECTUAL CLIMATE*

In the general soul searching which has taken place in American educational circles in the past few years, many different proposals have been advanced to improve the intellectual climate. Significant influences have been pointed out, but the influence of the physical setting is often overlooked or taken for granted. When the question is considered, the relationship is often unclear. Many people assume that education can take place in any kind of structure, while others beat the drums for some special kind of architecture. University Gothic, University Georgian, and Neo-Howard Johnson come to mind. To elaborate the taxonomy at this point would be pedantic; we wish, rather, to examine the relationships between architecture and education, between objects and symbols, between things and ideas.

In what ways does one influence the other, and in what ways *should* one influence the other? In this context, the question is: are buildings and other physical equipment of a university suited to the production of good intellectual climate?

* Reprinted from *School and Society* (February 25, 1961) by permission of *School and Society* and the co-author, Raymond H. Wheeler.

If we assume that intellectual growth and development are the prime goals of a college, then the equipment should be chosen and constructed to serve this end. The selections of buildings and equipment are based on various criteria. Some people prize modernity, others some concept of symmetry, and still others think buildings should have "character," which usually means anachronism. All of these can be loosely characterized as aesthetic judgments. On some campuses the aesthetics are looser than on others. Not infrequently, the person who gives (or controls) the money for a new building regards the building as a personal monument and bargains for the most prominent position and the most impressive façade he can obtain, regardless of the effect on the campus as a whole.

We think the chief criterion should be function: the buildings and equipment should aid and promote the intellectual activities, and not merely house them. Above all, they should not hamper them; and lest the reader dismiss this possibility too lightly, let us underline the assertion that few buildings are ever neutral; they tend to be for you or against you, and on most college campuses a large number are obstinately against.

Most people do not realize that in many cases physical form can limit, permit, and in extreme cases virtually determine the kinds of activities that can be engaged in. However, even the most obvious kinds of inquiry into these activities are often omitted when buildings are designed. Whether a door is at the front or back of a classroom can make far more difference to a teacher than an architect is likely to guess. (Back doors minimize disruptions.) The placement of a clock in the room can profoundly affect the degree of attention the class will maintain. (Clocks also should be in the back.) The ease of access to a laboratory, workroom, library,

or office strongly influences the traffic flow and, ultimately, the intellectual communication.

Propinquity, or nearness, greatly influences who talks
to whom and, conversely, who talks about whom. Marriage choices reflect this;[1] racial prejudice reflects this;[2]
voting behavior reflects this;[3] power and leadership are
distributed by it;[4] and scholarship or the lack thereof is
directly promoted or suppressed by propinquity on the
college campus.

Buildings are arbitrary divisions of space. Before a
wall is put up, we can argue whether a room should
accommodate 30 or 300 people, but once the bricks are
laid we are stuck with it.

Most poeple look upon a college campus as a set of
ivy-covered structures housing classrooms and labora-
tories. Offices are somehow tucked into corners, not
too far from related classrooms if possible. Libraries are
housed at some remote point where the view is good or
the memorial library looks well to visitors. Only the
athletic field is traditionally located with an eye toward
convenient parking. Sidewalks are put in where some
surveyor's transit told him they ought to go and not
where people have been observed to walk.

Physical setting often shows expectations. Classrooms
with elevated lecterns lead to lectures. Small tables surrounded by armchairs suggest discussions. Offices as
clean as a hospital and bare of books suggest that the

[1] M. R. Koller, *American Sociological Review,* 13: 613-616,
October, 1948.

[2] M. Jahoda and P. S. West, *Journal of Social Issues,* 7: 132-
139, Nos. 1 & 2, 1951.

[3] P. F. Lazarsfeld, B. Berelson, and H. Gaudet, "The People's
Choice" (New York: Columbia University Press, 1948), pp.
152-153.

[4] A. Bavelas, "Communication Patterns in Task-Oriented
Groups," Chap. 33, in D. Cartwright and A. Zander, "Group
Dynamics" (Evanston: Row, Peterson and Co., 1953).

university aims to be a well-run business rather than to promote scholarship and study. Too well-groomed a campus suggests a Parisian park, while there are a number of campuses that look more like country clubs and apparently serve as such. If you want students and faculty to pay attention to ideas and to love books and scholarly work, these things must be honored in the physical objects and campus structure as well as in the words of welcome traditionally uttered by deans and presidents.

One of the most important features of a good college education is rarely considered at all. Education has been defined as a scholar on one end of a log and a student on the other. The Greeks saw it as several students and a scholar walking. The British traditionally saw a tutor and his charge smoking and drinking tea in their digs. The common pervasive element is informal and congenial social contact among students and teachers, but apparently few colleges in America have sought self-consciously to provide physical surroundings calculated to maximize this congenial and informal contact.

You can't really talk in libraries, and for that matter, probably, you shouldn't. Student unions serve good purposes, but rarely that of intellectual discussion. A teacher's office can serve this purpose but is not often well adapted to it; and if it is used this way, such use interferes with other functions which the office should serve. By default, intellectual discussions which are so vital and demanding that they will be held despite all obstacles gravitate to the coffee shop, the rest room, and the neighborhood bar.

What can be done about it? In a British university, we have been told, planners seriously debated whether it would be better to use a fortuitous sum of money to hire a visiting lecturer or to build a rear stairway on one of the men's dorms. One line of argument was that the additional stairway would encourage men to visit each other's rooms, and the intellectual gains from this increase in communication might well be greater than the gain from the mere addition of another teacher.

In discussing the development and maintenance of social strata, Max Weber placed great emphasis on *commercium* and *connubium:* Whom you can eat with and whom you can marry.[5] Nomadic peoples have long used eating as both test and evidence of friendship. In every walk of life today, sharing food, drinks, and tobacco is both symbolic of camaraderie, and, by its popular equation with friendship, actually promotes general goodwill.

The sociology department in one midwestern university was laid out to include a "workroom" centrally located in the suite of offices and classrooms. The door was almost always open to all passersby and the coffee pot constantly ready. A most important intellectual advantage of this department over the others in the college was the open room and the coffee pot. This attracted sociology students at all hours of the day and part of the night, as well as teachers and students from half a dozen other departments. There were philosophers, geologists, economists, language people, and so on. Ostensibly, they wandered in to get a cup of coffee, but they remained to chat, discuss, and argue with whomever they met. Some days the argument started at eight o'clock in the morning with two graduate students, progressively involved five or six teachers on their off hours, and was kept up continuously all day, with various participants who came and went like people who sit in on a poker game and pass on their

[5] H. H. Gerth and C. Wright Mills, "From Max Weber" (New York: Oxford University Press, 1946), pp. 396 ff.

chairs when they have to leave. This interchange is an important part of a vigorous intellectual climate.

A well-designed university should include several different types of eating and lounging places, each with different decor and with well-defined differences in formality, suitable to different kinds of gatherings and available for choice almost any time. Of course, even the best considered floor plan can go astray. For instance, at one school the dean, from his British background, wanted a room for students to lounge in, and even suggested the name "bumming room." A large, well-lighted room was built, with wide doors near either end and picture windows facing the hallway so that an inviting air of informality would be achieved. But before the lounge furniture was installed, the building was opened for use. The janitors had a surplus of library tables and heavy wooden chairs on their hands so they shoved them into this room temporarily. Students, seeing the formal library furniture, arranged it into neat rows and proceeded to study. When some merrier itinerants wandered in and tried to hold a discussion, they were shushed and shamed into silence. This was a *study hall*—not by edict, not by intent, but by the unlucky accident of the presence of a bunch of unused library tables and chairs.

The point is this: material objects influence what gets done. There is some available knowledge about how to use this fact to advantage. It is equally evident that this is not easy, and it requires serious and constant attention. And it is painfully apparent that most of the time this is not given. Offices are distributed on the basis of prestige, departments even being split up so that department heads can have "Department Head's Offices"; libraries are built so that books are inaccessible or control over circulation is hazardous; stairs and walks installed in ways that do not encourage communication; and various kinds of non-intellectual considerations dominate the choice of plant and equipment.

Sometimes architects have curious notions of what is appropriate to a special discipline. At one midwestern university, a new building given to the mining school consisted of a four-story shaft with minute windows which immediately became christened the "four-story basement." It is just barely conceivable that mining should be taught in a mine, but what happened at a seaboard school where there is a marine biology department is indefensible. The new administration building was as well windowed as a goldfish bowl and, in keeping with this motif, the architect sank a large tank of goldfish in the floor. Unlike the people, however, the fish were not enclosed in glass, but in copper, which speedily killed off all the fish (as the marine biologist could have told the architect it would). The tank has been converted into a planter. The incident may be minor, but the point is not; although university faculties presumably are staffed with experts in many fields, they are among the last people consulted when new facilities are planned.

Every campus contributes its own exhibits to the architectual chamber of horrors. One school has a math classroom so dim that it is known locally as the Black Hole of Calculus. Music schools seem to inherit Charles Addams residences. We have an auditorium where the air-conditioner sounds as though it is equipped with Hollywood mufflers. Architectural influences which are not so direct are often surprisingly pervasive. At a midwestern school known largely for the excellence of its basketball teams, a student in music appreciation identified Strauss as the composer of the opera "Der Fielderhaus."

Lest we seem too prejudiced, it should be said that

architects are not the only ones who make mistakes. Their errors, though, are usually larger and more durable than those of other men. However, the same kind of nonchalant disregard of function is seen throughout the whole range of material objects we deal with in schools. Take the matter of seats. A fairly large minority of our people are left-handed, but this is never adequately recognized when equipment is set up in classrooms. To be sure, a half-hearted effort is made to keep around a couple of left-handed chairs, but any student of statistics can quickly point out how nearly impossible it is to predict how many should be kept in any one room, since left-handed people will not appear in precisely the same numbers, class after class. In large auditoriums there usually are no left-handed seats at all, just as there usually are none for people with larger-than-average bottoms. How simple it would be to build seats which are convertible so that the writing surface could be placed on either the left or right, and then anyone could sit anywhere. For seat size the problem may be more difficult, but who knows what intelligent solution might be obtained if the right people were asked? The point is that teaching and learning are somehow considered to take place alongside of, or in spite of, material surroundings. The audio-visual people at long last have convinced planners that a room with large windows must also have opaque shades if you hope to show movies, but this is a mere dent in a great wall of indifference.

Empty space should be considered, too. Among many primitive people a bit of vacant land (that is to say, land never used for productive operations such as hunting, gathering, grazing, or gardening) is left surrounding a village. The principle operating here is very simple and basic: spatial distance limits contacts among people. In the case of primitive tribes, cleared space around a village made surprise attacks difficult. Modern tribes also are aware of this. For example, colleges usually try to separate men and women's dorms with a bit of neutral space such as a grassy plot or an expanse of tennis courts. However, if this neutral ground is to eliminate surprise, concealment should be impossible. It is for this reason that the dean of women wants all tall bushes removed, just as early settlers cleared the ground around their log cabins.

Sometimes neutral ground has another function: it can be used to unite groups. Every college dean of students recalls with horror the winter snowball fight on land between rival men's dormitories, or the spring water fight on the commons between the women's and men's quadrangle. As Simmel puts it, "meetings of individuals which cannot take place on the territory of either group may be arranged to take place in a neutral area." [6] Early trading often took place at the periphery of villages or, in some cases, on neutral land at some point between tribal territories. Usually, Simmel claims, the existence of unoccupied space between groups is the most characteristic expression of potential antagonism. Translated into campus terms, this means that a small neutral area between people and departments can be designed to promote contact and unity, but that wide spatial separation of people and departments which should function together tends to produce friction and antagonism. You can't legislate informal social contacts; you can only conduce and permit them. For instance, at a big public housing project, it was discovered that women met each other principally at the laundry rather than at the professionally organized community center, which had been planned from the beginning to serve this

[6] N. J. Spykman, "The Sociology of Georg Simmel" (Chicago: University of Chicago Press, 1925), pp. 161-162.

function but didn't. These informal contacts even cut across racial lines because everyone had to use the laundry, whereas visiting in the community center was an obvious personal choice.

The water fountain in the factory and the galley in the ship both serve as centers of informal communication. In fact, in the Navy, the scuttlebutt or bubbler is synonymous with gossip. Zorbaugh[7] points out that the rooming house, in contrast to the boarding house, had no dining room or parlor. Therefore, there was no common meeting place where friendships could be initiated or maintained. Hence, anonymity and isolation prevailed. Perhaps this should be weighed by administrators who decry the apathy of student bodies.

In other cases,[8] the location of mailboxes, steps, and garbage cans defined communication patterns. People who have to use the same objects daily are naturally drawn into association. In one large rabbit-warren apartment development, the only person who regularly came to the front door was the mailman. Among other reasons people typically meet in the back is that this is where their children play. Thus, recreation often serves as the unifying interest among people of diverse ages, professions, and ways of life. If we must, for the sake of tradition, have quadrangles on modern college campuses, then let us at least use the central space for tennis courts, botanical gardens, and tea terraces so as to attract people and not merely divide them.

The sticks and stones bequeathed by outrageous fortune can leave more bumps on the minds of undergraduates than the windy words of degree-laden lecturers.

[7] H. W. Zorbaugh, "The Gold Coast and the Slum" (Chicago: University of Chicago Press, 1929), Chap. 4.

[8] L. Festinger, S. Schacter, and K. Back, "Social Pressures in Informal Groups" (New York: Harper, 1950), *passim*.

Bookshelves and ivy do not make a university, but they help. A book in hand is worth four in the stacks. Back doors are friendlier than front doors. The way to a man's mind is through his coffee cup. If you can't rub elbows, it is hard to rub minds.

Assorted
Social
Psychology

WE AND US

Although group is the central concept of most sociology and is widely used in other social sciences, it has no generally accepted definition. Many writers stress the organization of roles, whereas others discuss frequency and intimacy of association, sociometric preference, reciprocal influences, or combinations of these. One usual characteristic of social groups is the awareness by the individuals who make up the group that, together, they are distinguishable from the rest of society. We might even say that an essential step in the formation of a group is the recognition by the individuals that people may be thought of as belonging to categories, and that they personally belong to one or more of these.

Not all categories are groups. All males, for some purposes, form a category, as do all Negroes, all men with salaries above five thousand dollars, and so on. There may be groups corresponding to some of these categories, but the mere recognition that one might be categorized does not necessarily lead him to participate in a group. How does the awareness of similarities between oneself and others lead to the formation of a group?

There are two different, though not exclusive, kinds of awareness which can lead people to become a group. I call these WE awareness and US awareness because of an analogy between the grammatical use of the nominative and objective cases and the kinds of roles which the member ascribes to himself and the others in the group. As a number of people become a group, they become aware that they form a category, different from other people in some aspect which is important to them. They may regard this category as the active subject of some action or as the passive object of the action. WE *have done such and such,* or *Such and such has happened to* US. Often the latter view is antagonistic: *Look what those so-and-so's have done to* US! The grammatical distinction does not, of course, prove the psychological one. It merely expresses it.

John Thibaut[1] placed groups of boys in competitive game situations and then rigged the situations so that one group had marked success while the other had little success, received scant approval, and did the unpleasant work of the game. He expected the successful team to become more cohesive and the unsuccessful team less so. Cohesiveness actually increased in both, but not to the same degree, and included fewer members in the losing team.

In the terms I am using, Thibaut's losers regarded him (rightly) as the source of their difficulties, saw themselves as an US group which was being persecuted, and thus became more cohesive, while his winners viewed themselves as a WE group which succeeded, and were further attracted to each other.

When we think about groups in these terms, it appears that most of the research on group formation has been directed at factors producing WE awareness. WE awareness apparently develops most readily under conditions in which the collective efforts bring rewards. Or, to state it negatively, it has been shown that unre-

[1] John Thibaut, "An Experimental Study of the Cohesiveness of Underprivileged Groups," in Dorwin Cartwright and Alvin Zander (eds.) *Group Dynamics* (Evanston: Row, Peterson and Company) 1953, pp. 102-120.

warding group activities are disruptive; they produce hostility between members and scapegoating of specific individuals in order to absolve the group of failure and thus hold it together. WE refuse to admit that we have failed; failures are projected onto enemies or saboteurs. Successful cooperative action enhances WE awareness, while unsuccessful cooperative action destroys it. Individual competition within the group works against WE awareness, since the stress on individual excellence opposes the categorical attitude toward the self.

Any good coach can tell you the same thing. The boy who is too interested in his own score makes a poor team man, and for just this reason, some all-star teams never become teams at all. One of the main jobs of the coach is to keep his players thinking in terms of the team effort and the team victory and to play down the stress on individuals, which tends to take them out from under his control. Some coaches have developed elaborate myths and fancy names to try to build the group spirit. Remember the high spirited defensive football platoon called the Chinese Bandits?

There is a limit to the endurance of such a group, and the key to this was found in the early studies of group leadership. Groups which have a strong leader, such as a coach, often fall apart when he leaves. In my terms, these tend to be US groups. *He has* US *do so-and-so*. Groups which make their own decisions tend to see themselves in the WE form, and the departure of the leader is not so disruptive.

In conflict situations, whether on the sports field or elsewhere, people quickly recognize categorical relationships, and rival camps quickly form. On the other hand, pleasant experiences are not so likely to produce "US" awareness as the unpleasant ones. If a corporation declares an extra dividend, the stockholders are less likely to see themselves in an US relationship than if the company threatens bankruptcy. We do not need to band together when, individually, we are getting along well. *Misery loves company* is the proverbial statement of the US relationship.

At Fort Benning in 1943, a number of us were suddenly dropped from the Army Specialist Training Program (ASTP) for various reasons, none reflecting upon the efficiency of the individual cadets but because of a reorganization of the total program. Since being dropped was tantamount to being assigned to the infantry for combat, a strong and swift US awareness arose. ("*They can't do this to* US!") The droppees actively sought each other's sympathy and support. One man had informal contacts with headquarters and through these he discovered additional programs in Language and Area study for which a number of us made immediate application, and we set about tutoring each other to prepare for the examinations. Those of us who passed the screening exams solidified into a clearly identifiable and congenial group, whereas heretofore we had hardly known each other. The new group supplanted previous groups which had formed in fifteen weeks of training, and the basis was clearly the perception of new and important categorical relationships and the effective group behavior which followed. This new group, by the way, lost all interest in the current training procedures, and I recall with some amusement memorizing irregular French verbs while firing a light machine gun on the range.

After the war, in a married veterans' housing project at the University of Wisconsin, I found that cohesiveness varied greatly between the various apartment units, each of which housed six or more couples. The population was nearly homogeneous in age, income, marital status, occupational status of husbands, veteran status, and region of origin. Yet residents of some dorms

formed close-knit groups with high morale whereas
others did not. Because of the extreme lack of privacy,
the restricted living space, and other physical inconvenience, there was ample possibility for irritation; and
there was outright hostility in those dorms which did
not form organized groups. Few people remained neutral, whereas the residents in more private, urban apartment houses often do. My wife and I succeeded in organizing one dorm in which antagonisms had already
developed and produced a congenial group with high
morale. However, so far as the total population was
concerned, repeated efforts by us and others to organize
them had little success. Established dorm groups continued, and some persons from other dorms associated
with some of these, but no large overall group was
formed until a question of housing policy angered nearly
everyone in the project. It was a typical US relationship.

The problem may seem minor to outsiders and the
reaction petty, but it illustrates the kinds of norms which
develop in deprived populations. The typical apartment
consisted of a seven-by-nine-foot living room connected
to an identical bedroom by a five-by-nine-foot bath.
When it became possible to add to the number of apartments by converting other space, the new apartments
were planned to be a few square feet larger. Immediately, nearly everyone feared that newcomers would get
the larger apartments, and the general agitation and
unrest culminated in a mass meeting at which everyone
who wished had his say, and collective action was taken
supporting a plan to give the old residents prior claim
on the new apartments. The plan was accepted without
enthusiasm, however, because while it was conceded to
be fair, few stood to profit from it. Most people had gotten excited, feeling that they were being picked on, and
they had tried to do something constructive, and now

only a few were going to get any benefit from all the activity. The temporary cohesiveness vanished and never again was there any sort of over-all group spirit, even of an US type. The kinds of group success which had welded some of the dorms into vigorous, proud units could not be managed on a larger scale.

Large groups which are to be held together require constant attention to communication and organization, and almost automatically a professional leadership class must emerge. Moreover, in order to get people to join and stay with a group, there must be something in it for them, either defense or gain. Mere congeniality is not enough, unless there is outside pressure and isolation. A persecuted minority may have to stick together for congeniality since friends are not available outside, but most people in modern society have a variety of contacts and many potential friends. It takes more than mere friendliness to cement a group.

A group which forms on the basis of US awareness may fail to develop WE feelings and may dissolve when actions are attempted. For instance, in Cincinnati, a local agitator got people worked up over the proposed introduction of fluorides into the drinking water. Some people thought this was a threat to their health and formed a group opposing the plan. They were apparently solidly together in the US phase, but dissent arose when they tried to plan positive activities. Some members viewed the group as a generalized "anti" movement to censor textbooks, fight un-American activities, and engage in other reactionary operations. Immediately, other adherents resigned because, while they identified with the other members of the group in viewing themselves as a category of persons being persecuted, they did not identify with the others in the action program which emerged.

This contrast between the two types of group awareness is borne out in studies of political movements in which control and consensus may be maintained temporarily by a leader who focusses attention on what is being done to US, only to disintegrate when WE have to act. If a convincing transition can be made from the passive US situation to the active and rewarding WE situation, cohesiveness and control are secured. WE and US feelings are not necessarily interdependent, nor are they necessarily mutually exclusive.

Shortly after I had formulated these ideas in the present terms, I had a chance to give them an informal test. It was hardly an experiment, but just one of those happy chances in which a sociologist can get a closer look at a process he has been regarding abstractly. Essentially I wanted to see how readily you could induce a group to shift from an US to a WE form, from a passive group which was letting itself be led to a group which would actively take over from the leader and direct itself. Obviously the decision must come from the members of the group, and it would not come if the leader were doing what they wanted done. People don't change something that works to their satisfaction; I would have to make them dissatisfied and, at the same time, self-confident and congenial.

The opportunity to test my formulations came when an organization called Fellowship House asked me to lead a study group in the interest of improving morale in the organization. The course was announced with the ambiguous statement that it would deal with group processes, and another member of the organization and I were named as leaders. My co-leader made it clear to the group that she would only handle details of announcements, meeting arrangements, and the like, and that content would be left to me.

Since the group knew I was a teacher, they expected a class, conducted along university lines. To their surprise, they were pushed into two groups of seven and eight each to discuss various topics, and then the whole group participated in a general critique session which was rather permissively lead. The discussion topics began with the very personal (*What I was like when I got out of grade school*), moving by degrees away from the self toward group interests. My hunch was that most people can talk readily about what they "were" and derive narcissistic satisfaction without feeling that they too intimately reveal what they "are." At the same time, the others should feel that they know the speakers better, since they are vicariously growing up with them, and the comparison of experiences and interests should lead to the discovery of similarities or a "categorical attitude" toward the self and the others. This happened.

With minimal leadership, I expected that the members should discover some simple facts about group processes themselves, and with growing cohesiveness but lacking outside leadership, they should eventually develop their own task orientation and take charge of the group themselves. I predicted that this would take place on the fourth of the five meetings and that on the fifth I could retire completely to the role of observer. Things went as predicted, except that I underestimated my people and they took over at the end of the third session.

The transition in group awareness was apparent and others in the group commented on it. The first session went as directed, and most people seemed to enjoy it. At the second, they asked me for more direction, and when it was not forthcoming, they adopted some clumsy methods of control which had accidentally emerged in the first session, with the result that discussions bogged down badly. Comparison of the nearly identical experiences in the two groups pointed up general principles, such as size, seating arrangements, roles of discussants, and control devices. Both in the critique following this session and throughout the third one, suspicious and challenging comments were hurled at me, venting dissatisfactions and trying to make me lead.

"You're supposed to be the leader here, what do we do now?" "Why don't you make so-and-so shut up? He talks too much!" "Do you think we're a good group?" "Is this group as good as the other one?" "Do you think we're getting along as fast as we ought to?" "Where are we supposed to be going, anyhow?" "I think this guy doesn't really care whether we get anything out of this or not. He's just using us for a bunch of guinea pigs. We'll all wind up in an article somewhere!"

I was politely evasive and left them to answer their own questions, in turn interjecting some of my own. By the end of the third meeting, the members warmly agreed that the meetings had been pleasant and stimulating, and that they understood each other much better, but they felt that all of this new congeniality and cooperativeness should be put to some purpose. Before I offered any suggestions for the next meeting, they asked why they couldn't devote the remaining meetings to discussing practical plans for improving Fellowship House, and the fourth and fifth meetings proceeded along that line.

The transition from an US group (*He is going to teach* US *about group processes*) to a WE group (*What are* WE *going to do to improve Fellowship House?*) was accomplished. By first gathering a group *vis-a-vis* a leader whose profession commanded their respect, and then simultaneously encouraging their recognition of similar experiences and interests and allowing them to use the leader as a target for collective dissatisfactions with the group activities, they were "led" to take for their own the role which they had originally imputed to the leader, and WE did whatever was accomplished.

The procedure makes sense theoretically, if the ideas in this essay are correct, and in this one test instance at least it came off somewhat as planned. There is a cautionary note to anyone who wants to use it, however. If you want the group to become self-directing, you must let them go their own way. You can't use this approach to manipulate them without their knowing it. And once they have taken charge of themselves, you must not try to take the credit for what they accomplish. The whole procedure is designed to convince them that they don't need you at all.

To sum up, it appears that WE awareness occurs principally when some collective action is rewarding. US awareness appears in unpleasant situations in which the collectivity is the object of mistreatment by fate or by particular individuals. Both unpleasant and pleasant experiences may give rise to groups depending upon, among other things, how the relationships between self, situation, and category are perceived. If what we collectively do is pleasant, or what is done to us collectively is unpleasant, and it looks as if we can do something about it, we are likely to form a group. Under some circumstances, passive US groups may be transformed into active WE groups, with good morale and good prospects for practical accomplishments. A full and formal statement of the hypothesis is as follows: Formation and perseverance of a group is most likely to occur when a collection of persons becomes aware that they are members of a category which has experienced an unpleasant situation and when, on the basis of their common awareness, they collaborate in successful collective action to overcome it. X was done to US, and WE did Y.

THE SOCIOLOGY
OF HUMOR
AND VICE VERSA

Man has been variously defined as the rational animal, the social animal, and the political animal by writers trying to relate him to his confrères in the animal kingdom and yet to distinguish certain of his traits from theirs. With equal justification, we might redefine man as the humorous animal.

Man's appreciation of humor has apparently limitless extension. All tribes laugh. Throughout history, there have been individuals and groups occupied with the production of humor in a professional capacity as clowns, jesters, playwrights, or whatever such roles the particular society afforded. Man has long used humor as a means of gaining various socially defined ends. This is especially clear in politics where, from the satire of Aristophanes' *The Clouds* to the latest wisecracks about the President, humor of all kinds has been employed in polemics against political opponents.

If we accept the proposition that man generally attempts to be rational, we may safely assume that as long as there have been jokes and jokesters, there have also been men who wondered what was so funny; however, most of the significant attempts to explain what was funny from a technical standpoint have been made within relatively recent times.

The work on humor has been done for the most part by psychologists and philosophers. Some sociologists have dabbled around the edges, mostly concerned with particular situations giving rise to humor or with the uses of humor as a weapon in racial and minority disputes. No one has attempted an overall analysis of broad categories of humor (such as the joke, the cartoon, and the wisecrack) in the light of a carefully elaborated sociological or socio-psychological theory. It is just not the sort of thing sociologists officially favor.

I read a paper on jazz in the first section on Sociology of the Arts ever to be offered at a national convention, and that section was a long time coming. I don't expect to live long enough to witness a section on humor, which is a great pity. The contributions would be interesting, since there is great opportunity for controversy in this field, although they might not be as funny as the traditional forensics over methodology.

If sociologists are reluctant to discuss humor at their meetings, they are even less willing to employ it either as a vehicle or a grace of presentation. There have been few sociologists who would deliberately present an argument in a humorous way, and be it sadly noted that when they spoke, most people came to laugh but not to ponder.

I once submitted a satire to a meeting chairman who is also a close friend of mine. He rejected it, saying that he had enjoyed it thoroughly, but that he once saw a very funny paper by another sociologist die a dreadful death at the hands of the convention, so he thought he had better get a more serious paper for his program. That is the nub of the problem, he could not risk *his* program. Editors love to read a funny essay themselves, but few will risk publishing one in *their* journal. It would seem that among sociologists humor is to be enjoyed only clandestinely, like sex. One of the funniest things about sociologists is that they are so afraid of being funny. I am sure that this is the basic reason they changed the name of the national organization from the American Sociological Society to the American Sociological Association. Somehow, sociologists have been afraid to tackle anything that was not deadly serious with the result that the humor at most meetings is unplanned.

This is curious because in general, sociologists probably have about as good a sense of humor as, say psychologists, and better than most chemists and physicists. A number of them are known socially as raconteurs, but once they ascend the meeting platform they assume as serious a mein as an English judge and defy anything funny to happen. In curious contrast, there is now a slight vogue for cartoons and jokes in introductory texts, most of which are still not very funny.

Anthropologists are less stuffy. Scudder Mekeel and I shared a curiosity about humor and used to try to figure out what made jokes funny. I recall one of his experiences with American Indian humor. He had associated for some time with Sioux. A little later he visited some Crow. When the Crow heard that he had lived with the Sioux they assumed mock annoyance and said, "Listen, mister, don't you know they are our enemies? We used to eat Sioux for breakfast!" During his stay he was invited to a kind of men's club meeting in the long house, and the highlight of the evening's entertainment came when one of the Crow appeared dressed up as a Sioux and strode around boasting about what great men the Sioux were and how cowardly the Crow were, and how many Crow scalps he had taken and how many coup counts he had made. (The coup count was a demonstration of extreme bravery, and consisted of sneaking up on an armed enemy and instead of killing him just tapping him with a little decorated stick and reciting an appropriate formula. The main trick, of course, was to come back from such a performance alive.)

This burlesque received such a hand that Scudder thought he would get into the act. There was an extra lodge pole lying nearby, a sapling several inches in diameter and about fifteen feet long, and it occurred to him to use it as a coup stick. So, he got up, hefted it with all eyes on him, staggered up to the chief, poked him in the chest with this undersized telephone pole and recited the Sioux coup count formula. There was a polite, "Heh, heh, heh," from all hands and it was painfully obvious that he had made a mistake. Ever try to get rid of a telephone pole? Embarrassing.

After the party, Scudder asked one of the Crow what went wrong. "Look," he said, "you laughed when your friend pretended to be a Sioux and went through all that nonsense. Now, you call me a Sioux, and I thought if I took a coup count on the chief that would be a good joke." "You're right," replied the Crow, "it would be, but you made one mistake. You shouldn't have used something big like that lodge pole. You should have used something very small. You could have taken out a match, and broken it in half, and then split it, and used that. That would have been very funny."

Most such theories are never tested, but Scudder had a chance to test that one. A few weeks later, he met another group of Crow, and while they were chatting it came out that he had lived with the Sioux. They started the same sort of banter as before: "Why we had so many Sioux scalps we used them for rugs!" At this point Scudder borrowed a match, broke it and split it, with all the men watching curiously to see what he was up to, and then quickly before any could step back he took four coup counts in rapid succession. Result? They howled with laughter and thought he was one of the funniest men they had ever met. Exaggeration seems to be a characteristic of humor everywhere, but the direction and manner of the exaggeration are clearly limited by culture.

One of the differences between British and American humor hinges on the kind of exaggeration employed. Many American jokes proceed by overstatement, and so do some British jokes, but the British also often use understatement, a device rare on these shores.

Jokes of peoples who have often been persecuted or oppressed frequently have a peculiar, insidious way of sliding up to the point, so that the listener discovers the joke himself, rather than having it thrown at him. This is true, for example, of many Jewish and Negro jokes. A classic example is the Jewish marriage broker story in which the *schadchen* is extolling the fine points of the girl, amid suspicious inquiries by the boy's father. Finally the father says, "Now, look. The girl you describe has too many virtues for the bride price you say they will ask. Be truthful, there is something wrong with her which we have not been able to guess. What is it?" To which the *schadchen* replies, "Well, maybe she could be just a little bit pregnant."

This outrageous satire is characteristic of jokes about a special group told within the group. Another Jewish joke has the grandmother in a supermarket questioned by a stranger who admires the two little boys with her. "What lovely children. Your grandchildren?" Grandmother nods, beaming. "How old are they?" "The doctor is six and the lawyer is four." Only a Jew who is ambivalent about the intense family ambition for learning forced upon him can fully appreciate this joke. Jewish humor is especially fascinating because of the diverse elements which feed into it: love of learning, persecution, ambition, chicanery, family bonds, migration, mobility, and so on. Of course, specific jokes about real or reputed characteristics of Jews will translate to any other group with the same reputed characteristics. Many jokes about saving money are equally applicable to Scotsmen, the other chief target of the stinginess stereotype in our society. A curious side effect of this stereotype is that many Jews feel obliged to refute it by excessive generosity, but few Scots do! Scots revel in telling such jokes on themselves. Most people do not know enough about Chinese to turn these jokes toward them.

Stereotypes must be plausible if they are to be used in jokes, because part of the effect of a joke comes from the speed of its development. If some concept is used which requires study or invites critical examination, the development of the joke is slowed down. About the only thing which will make it funny then is the sheer ridiculousness of its pretensions. An example of this is the story about the man who comes up to a friend and says, "Hey, did you hear the story about the two Jews. . . ." At this point his friend interrupts and says, "Listen, you damned anti-Semite, all I ever hear from you is jokes about Jews. Don't you know any other kind of jokes?" "All right, all right. Here's another one. There are these two Chinese walking down the street when one of them turns to the other and says, 'Say Abie. . . .'" For a more sophisticated audience, especially a Jewish audience, the joke is improved by naming the Chinese "Milton." This again is the "inside" joke, since all Jews know that Milton is an upward-mobile substitute for Moses or Moishe.

The use of inside jokes by outsiders is generally dangerous. A Jew may needle a Jew but an Irishman may not. A Negro may kid a Negro about segregation, but a white man may not. Very often inside humor is so bitter that outsiders are shocked when exposed to it. When I was in Iran during World War II, a G.I. brought our dance band a parody on the song "Don't Fence Me In," with the title "Don't Send Me Home." When you understand that men had been there as much as three years in temperatures up to 146 degrees, with poor food and other miserable conditions, just the title is shocking. The lyrics were worse. We in the band thought it was pretty funny but were afraid to use it. However, after a suitable introduction to explain that we were only kidding, we tried it, with an appropriately raucous vocal chorus and accompaniment. (Today we would call it rock and roll!) It was a huge success and became the hit of the command, but when soldiers sent copies home, their parents were horrified. This sort of extreme and bitter satire has been called "gallows humor" and one of the few articles on humor published by a sociological journal deals with this type.

A fundamental concept in social psychology is that of the frame of reference, and related to it, the reference group. These twin notions are highly useful in examining jokes. Many jokes derive their effect by contrasting two different frames of reference in which something which would be appropriate to one is mistaken and inappropriate to the other. Let's look at a few simple examples.

> There was a young man from the city,
> Who saw what he thought was a kitty.
> He gave it a pat, but it wasn't a cat,
> And we buried his clothes out of pity.

The man from the city, with an urban frame of reference, wrongly defined the real situation involving the skunk, with disastrous results. Other things are involved, of course. Perhaps the reader identifies with the rural population and exults when vaunted urban superi-

ority takes a fall. The joke may be more generally classi-
fied as sadistic, like the stock example of the fat man
and the banana peel. In addition, the story is not nearly
so funny (*if* funny at all) in prose. However, the most
basic element involved is that of the frame of reference
and the definition of the situation.

There is a hoary military joke about the colonel who
was standing on a hill watching the progress of the battle
through his binoculars when his orderly, who was standing beside him, noted incredulously, "Why, Colonel,
your knees are shaking!" The Colonel coldly replied,
"Young man, if you were half as afraid as I am, you
would have run off an hour ago!"

Here are two people, operating from contrasting
frames of reference, defining the same situation variously. It becomes humorous when we see that the apparent positions of strength and weakness are reversed
when the frames of reference and their resulting definitions are correctly understood.

Here is another. A haberdasher from the Bronx by
the name of Ginsberg had made considerable money
in business, and recognizing his limited cultural background decided to take a trip to Europe. On the ship
he was seated at mess opposite a Frenchman. At the
first meal, the Frenchman bowed low from the waist
and said *"Bon appetit!"*; in reply, our man stuck out
his hand and said, "Ginsberg!" This procedure was repeated from meal to meal. Toward the end of the voy-
age, Ginsberg was remarking to a shipboard acquaintance about the various people on board and observed
that the Frenchman he ate with was a charming fellow,
very polite, but had a poor memory. "Doesn't speak
any English. Fellow by the name of Bon Appetit." "Why
you ignorant provincial, that's not his name, and he's
not introducing himself either. That's just French for
good appetite. He's wishing you a hearty meal." Gins-

berg, abashed and embarrassed at this exposure, determined to right himself in the eyes of his fellow passengers. At the next meal he arrived early at table and when the Frenchman approached, Ginsberg bowed low from the waist and murmured, *"Bon appetit!"*, at which the Frenchman grinned broadly, stuck out his hand and replied, "Ginsberg!"

In this story, the reader appreciates from the start that Mr. Ginsberg, due to limited educational opportunities, has a limited frame of reference which leads him to define the table situation in a way which is socially inadequate. This is a little different from the problem of our erstwhile friend from the city, where the real situation was demonstrated empirically. In the military story, we contrasted two frames of reference, or the definitions of different subjects, in order to understand the difference in their behavior, and suddenly reevaluated their respective bravery. In the shipboard story, the phenomenon in question is social, and here, more obviously than in the more strictly "natural" situations, we may be unable to arrive at any "real" situation on which we could generally agree. Although we would generally accept the proposition that if people believe things are real, they are real in their consequences, we are here treating that definition itself as the basic datum and its relation to the situation is the crucial point. We try to maintain our neutrality and just compare the subject's definition to that generally held in the society in which the joke is told, without regard to its "reality." Our early realization of the inadequacy of Ginsberg's definition may not be humorous unless we dislike Jews. The joke becomes funny, however, when we comprehend that the Frenchman held precisely the same kind of inadequate definition for similar reasons, and the American is no more provincial than the European.

Another story depending on a verbal misunderstanding is the one about the three deaf Englishmen on the train. The first looked about and asked, "I say, is this Wimberly?" The second said, "No, this is Thursday," to which the third agreed heartily, "So am I! Let's get off and have a drink!" A further point for the understanding of this story is that in our society many people do not regard puns as funny. Consequently, on hearing "Thursday," we defined the joke as having been completed, and a poor one at that. The successive, second pun is rare and is not included in our general frame of reference. As it turns out, the joke is actually on us for having wrongly defined the present situation within which the joke is being told.

Another example is the Irishman who was working on the sewer in a red-light district when a Protestant clergyman entered one of the houses. He turned to his helper and said, "There, now! Isn't that just what I've always said about them Protestants, their clergy and all! Oh, the black shame of it!" Only a few moments later, a Jewish rabbi followed suit. "Yes, and it goes for them, too. Birds of a feather, y'know." In course of time, the parish priest appeared and entered the same house. "Well, what do you know about that," said Pat. "One of the poor girls must be sick!"

Here we laugh at the facility with which our stereotyped Irishman produces diametrically opposed definitions of similar situations in order to maintain the prejudice essential to his frame of reference.

Another story concerns a man who is honor bound to avoid certain forms of speech. He realizes that without using these forms or something equally emphatic, he will not communicate to the other. The way he resolves the dilemma is the crux of the joke. A minister was riding on a train, reading his morning devotions to himself as was his custom. Across the aisle, a hardened old reprobate spied the Bible and muttered darkly, "I don't believe a word in that book." No reply. He said more audibly, "I don't believe a *word* in that book." Still no response. He leaned across the aisle, tapped a finger emphatically on the opened page and fairly shouted, "I DON'T BELIEVE A WORD IN THAT BOOK!" The minister turned to him, smiled sweetly, and said "Then will you please go to Hell quietly?"

These are just a few examples, and analyzed by just a few concepts. The shift of frame of reference in which what we thought was true is suddenly shown to be false is a basic element in jokes, at least in our culture. Many jokes end on a tag line in which one of the characters says to the other, "Oh, thank Heaven, I thought you said. . . ." We will laugh if we disagree with his obvious relief. This may be either because we see no difference in the two situations or because we feel the one he chooses is worse than the one he rejects. An example is the man who hears a speaker predict the end of the world and says in fright: "When did you say?" "One hundred million years." "Oh, thank heaven, I thought you said a million!"

In every culture there are things which are sufficiently sacred to be very funny if surreptitiously joked about, and there are other things too sacred for most people to dare joke about at all. Deformities come in for humor but vary widely from culture to culture. We laugh at obesity, but we see nothing funny about hunchbacks, although in other times and other cultures they have been thought funny. We have many jokes about deafness, in which the deficiency confuses frames of reference, but very few about blindness, which to us is somehow too tragic to joke about. Yet deafness is more disruptive to personality than blindness. Most blind people are fairly chipper and outgoing. They tend to be shallow because of the difficulty of intensive learning with so few props for memory, but they are, as a category, well adjusted and self-confident. The deaf, in contrast, are often suspicious, withdrawn, and morose. Nonetheless, our stereotypes permit deaf jokes without end. Sometimes deafness is merely a vehicle, and the deaf man stumbles onto a profound truth or performs like the delphic oracle. One joke of this sort concerns the man who takes his deaf uncle to church. "There's the preacher," he whispers. "Eh?" says the uncle. "You say he's a *teacher?*" "No, he's the *preacher*. He's the son of the Bishop!" "Yes, aren't they all!"

Mekeel and I concluded that one of the most striking features of sexual stories in our culture was the notion of personal deficiency. Most American sexual stories deal in one way or another with sexual frustration. Many deal with organ inferiority. They are full of hostility, and the punch line of the joke takes the form of *sartor resartus,* or the hunter gets hunted. This sudden switch of bottom dog to top dog is also seen in non-sexual jokes as well. A classic example is the one about the guy who slashes at the other with a razor. "Missed me!" cries the second. "Huh, uh! Just wait 'til you try to shake your head!" When we recall that this story is usually told with Negro characters, the content also shows elements of stereotype, such as the penchant for the razor as the weapon of choice for dueling, and the indirection in the tag line, which I attribute to the humor of oppressed people.

The transvaluation theme can feature as the hero any one who is supposed to be subservient to another. Terse truths may come not only out of the mouths of babes and sucklings, but from colored maids, Irish ditch-diggers, enlisted men in the army, prisoners at the dock, commoners speaking up to His Lordship, henpecked husbands to overbearing wives, and so on endlessly. Virtue made vice is often the turn, as when the teacher scolds the pupil for not knowing all the presidents.

"When I was your age I could name every one!" "When you were my age there were only three or four!"

A good example of this is the story of the southern Negro in court for fighting. The judge asks him why he hit the man. "Well, judge, he called me a black sonofabitch, so I hit him. Judge, if someone called you a black sonofabitch, wouldn't you hit him?" "I don't think so," says the judge judicially. "In the first palce I'm not black." "Well," says the Negro, "if he called you the kind of sonofabitch you *are* wouldn't you hit him?" Many other jokes involve this same kind of selective editing of an objectionable or incorrect description. For example, "You just think I'm a stupid little idiot." "Oh, no! You're not so little." This is basically a funny device, but it has been reduced to a formula and so many radio and television gags have been written from it that it no longer occasions surprise. In other words, the variations which are possible are included in our original frame of reference, and thus we do not find them funny.

It is not necessary to reverse completely the social standings of the opponents in a joke for it to be funny. If one person is tentatively accepted as being higher in status than the other, then showing them as even up is a kind of moral victory and serves almost as well. For example, a Catholic priest met one of his Irish parishioners working under an Italian foreman and kidded him, saying "Hey, Pat, how do you like your Dago boss?" To this Pat replied, "Fine, Father, and how do you like yours?" We can make a charitable double assumption that the priest is Irish and the foreman is a good Catholic, so that it all becomes an inside joke. With modifications, this same story could become an outside joke with bitter, polemical force.

A wartime story pits two minorities against the prejudiced majority, and employs the re-editing gambit as well. In the story, a Southern lady calls the army camp to invite six soldiers for Sunday dinner. When asked whether she has any preferences, she says no, and then as an afterthought, says, "But no Jews. I just can't stand Jews!" Comes Sunday and six, handsome, Negro G.I.'s appear. She splutters, "There must be some mistake!" "Oh, no, ma'am, Captain Goldberg never makes mistakes." We must assume that she is forced by her own standards of etiquette to feed them, otherwise, the force of the joke turns back on them, and ultimately on the Captain as well.

Obviously, we draw curtains on such jokes at conventional points, frame our vignettes at agreed-upon borders, and know when the inning is supposed to be over. We have learned this from our culture, and it often puzzles outsiders. Franz Adler tells about the multi-lingual comedian who was telling jokes in several languages on shipboard to a cosmopolitan audience and said, "Now I will tell German jokes and I will make a little sign with my hand like so when I come to the end." It may be prejudice on my part, but to me most German jokes do seem heavy and ponderous. They seem to work hard at their humor, in contrast to, say, the Italians, who sort of toss it out as they go by.

Mark Twain distinguished between comic, witty, and humorous stories and attributed these types to different nationalities, but his definitions do not seem to hold up.[1] He seems to have been better at doing it than discussing it, which is common among artists of all kinds.

Most of the jokes discussed so far presume only that the hearer is acquainted with common stereotypes and common customs. There is a further range of jokes so local in meaning that they are not at all funny to outsiders because of the tedious translations required, and

[1] Mark Twain, *How to Tell a Story* (New York: Harper, 1904).

another range of jokes which demand the intimate knowledge of two or more cultures. Both serve limited audiences for obvious reasons. Many musicians' jokes are hardly comprehensible to non-musicians, which is also true of jokes from other sub-cultures. What sense could a hill-billy from Arkansas make of a joke which has two men on a raft crying: "Water, Water" and a third crying "Seltzer, seltzer!"? Equally nonplussed would be a Brooklynite faced with the question: "Did you turn the chickens?" Probably each will suspect that the other is saying something dirty!

Jokes involving contrasting sexual mores are very funny to those acquainted with the different standards but are apt to be perplexing or insulting to those who do not. A mild example of this cosmopolitan brand of humor finds two youngsters strolling in Greenwich Village when they are met by a friend who sings out happily: "Hi there, kids! How do you like married life?" In alarm they whisper, "Shh! The neighbors don't know we are married!" This is an old joke, retreaded for various epochs and settings, just as old military jokes are reissued with each war, and some drunk jokes have been re-run as narcotic jokes, bop musician jokes, or beatnik jokes.

Incidentally, of all the many bop jokes, most of which were merely ridiculous analogies with tag lines like "Dig that crazy music stand," one joke stands out as capturing the real intensity and singular interest of the bopper. Two cats are walking down the Street in the Apple when a despondent citizen leaps from the tenth floor to his death on the sidewalk in front of them. One turns to the other and says, "G flat." Don't dig around for any hidden meanings; the point is simply that all the bopper cared for in this world was sounds. The suicide is only incidental to the story, to underscore the degree of abstraction which the musician employs. An auto horn would do as well but would have less shock value. By using a suicide, this joke approaches but does not really become a "sick joke." In the latter, the real joke is on the hearer, as it is with most puns. These jokes exploit the listener, and telling them is a kind of aggressive behavior similar to writing dirty words on fences. There is a fine line between satire, which must defile and attack, and the mere desecration which characterizes most of the sick jokes. The latter are not new, although their naming indicates a greater sophistication on the part of the public, which has begun to categorize some kinds of humor. Shakespeare and Dickens both used sick jokes and for about the same purposes as we use them today. As with all humor, when the pattern becomes too apparent, it loses effect. A parade of puns is annoying and a parade of sick jokes revolting.

This discussion, diffuse as it is, merely scratches the surface. There are innumerable insights which sociologists could offer about the nature of humor if this were recognized as a legitimate field of sociological endeavor. Moreover, as both the psychoanalysts and the anthropologists already know, studying humor can give a great many insights into other phases of the life of any people. If you know what people joke about, you can guess what worries them. Perhaps this is why sociologists are so guarded about studying humor or using humor in professional circles. They have much to worry about and one does not mention ropes in the house of a man who has been hanged.

UPWARD SKIDDING
AND THE AUTOMATIC
VALUE SHIFT

Americans are traditionally upward-mobile. Horatio Alger may not be regarded as a true prophet, but he certainly expressed our most fervent desire. Upward mobility is pleasant, profitable, and moral as well. "Going up in the world" feeds us better, clothes us more radiantly, surrounds us with a "better class" of friends, and helps us find our true identity, to "become somebody." Going up proves our sound judgment, good character, hard work, and, in an earlier day, divine blessing. Going down, on the other hand, is the evidence of mistakes, inability, bad luck, or the vengeance of God. Everyone wants to go up; no one wants to go down. We have long cherished the illusion that we choose to go up, and are only forced to go down. It is time we wake up to the fact that Skid Row is actually a two-way street.

This idea is very hard to grasp for several reasons. First of all, in looking backward over our own lives, the admission, if we have moved up, that this might have been a mistake in choice or that we were coerced into it by outside forces is embarrassing or painful, depending upon how sharply we see it. Secondly, young people, who are still young enough to make a choice, have insufficient experience on which to base it; and while their parents may have had the experience, it is not very often shared with their children in any meaningful way. It merely provides anecdotes to attest how far the old man has come and to imply how much farther his children will go. Thirdly, nearly all of the current ideologies support a contrary point of view, and anyone who dares suggest that there is something worth seeking other than upward mobility is cast into outer darkness along with beatniks, bopsters, and other obvious sore losers.

In an earlier day, the Alger myth used to be accompanied by the Franklinism that we should save toward the attainment of worthwhile ends. Furthermore, the worthwhile ends were all defined in rather standard and unchanging fashion, so that once you got them, you had them, and that was that. Saving for a rainy day really meant saving up to buy a standardized umbrella and roof. But today, many people regard any little shower as a rainy day, and the mark of good judgment is no longer to come in out of the rain, but rather to come on in, the water's fine!

In the early days, acquiring riches did not endanger the personal integrity of the Calvinist, because he was not permitted to consume them. For him, using money meant investing it, ploughing it back into the business or bestowing it for good works. But today getting ahead (*i.e.,* getting richer) is a real, though artfully disguised, threat to the contemporary hedonist who has adopted the "fun morality" simply because he *must* use his money: that is to say, he must eat it, drink it, drive it, wear it, live it up, and in the process be excited by it, if not genuinely made merry. The tired television plot of the man who has a fortune dropped in his lap under the stipulation that he must spend it all as rapidly as possible is really a contemporary Miracle and Morality play, and we think it should only happen to Everyman.

We have made a business of simulating success. Deficit financing is a way of rejecting not only the limitations of the past but of the present as well. In consuming today what we hope to earn tomorrow, we live in what, to parallel Kurt Lewin, we might call the economic present. A sample case might run like this. As sales manager of a large firm, I would like to own a fancier house and a bigger car. To buy these at my present salary and position would be financially dangerous. However, if I were sure of getting the vice-presidency, it would be safe. Therefore, if I go ahead and get them now, this will help me get the vice-presidency, because it will give me the confidence and incentive I need to get it, and it will show everyone else how confident and capable I am. The most sobering fact about this is that in the *folie à foule* that is modern big business, it very often works!

The ideology of upward mobility is so firmly insinuated into our moral fibre that most people cannot perceive that there is anything wrong with it at all. Like opiate addicts, they seek to cure any pains by a greater injection of the drug. If they begin to pant and stagger as they run, they are convinced that equilibrium can be maintained if they only run a little faster, and that the air is better nearer the top. Not every group, however, is so naive. Jazz musicians, with all of their personal eccentricities, are coldly and analytically perceptive of this point. They like money and enjoy pleasure as much as any members of our society, but they draw a neat sharp line between being commercial and "going commercial." Being commercial means that a man is making money or selling. Good for him. Going commercial means that he has prostituted his abilities and plays music he knows to be bad just to get a few more lousy dollars. He is no longer selling, he has sold out.

Paraphrasing C. Wright Mills' analysis of the white collar man, we observe that the upward skidder sells his personality all day long to try to get enough money to buy a little piece of it back at night. However, in these inflationary times, he often finds at night that the price has gone up. He has pressed his face so hard into the mask that the mask won't come off. "We tend to become what we pretend to be," and the skidder, trying so hard to appear to be something he covertly thinks he is not, becomes something, but he knows not what. By trying to be just a little bit phoney in order to become successful, he winds up as a successful, big phoney.

Another way of putting it is to say that the man who is skidding upward is constantly *nouveau riche*. The first things he has to learn how to do are to say hello and goodbye. His rapid succession of friends are devalued into contacts, sometimes contacts of an electrical momentariness. He cannot hold any person tightly, even including his wife; he might outgrow her. He never really owns anything; he only rents it, regardless of how the legal title reads. His suits never fit him from use, they are newly fitted onto him. (Our slang perceptively identifies changing roles with changing hats, and calls the stable and unpretentious personality an old shoe.) Most important of all, the skidder can never regard any geographic locality as home; he may only view it as passing scenery. He can never stop to feel the dirt beneath his feet, only the small, well-cushioned seat of the vehicle that rushes him along. He can never stop; he can only be stopped.

A good friend of mine who was stationed in Japan after World War II discovered that the price of Scotch in the PX was ridiculously low, and realizing that this was an error, he set about trying to drink it as rapidly as he could, so as to consume as much as possible before someone discovered and corrected the mistake. The only trouble was, he found that the manufacturers could make it faster than he could drink it and he nearly became an alcoholic. The example, although unusual, is not far-fetched. If you absorb enough of any kind of luxury, it becomes difficult to take it or let it be.

When a college professor writes like this, of course, he lays himself open to various charges. Sour grapes is a good one, because about the only time he is tempted by luxury is at a bookman's party at a convention or when some unscrupulous parent tries to buy a grade for an indolent son. Even then, the best offering price I ever received was a couple of baseball tickets! Perhaps the charge can be made that the teacher solves the moral problems of life in the real world by getting himself to a nunnery. Perhaps some teachers are skidders too, except that on the campus the slope is less steep. Socrates' debate about whether to drink the hemlock is still an instructive one. You recall that he concluded he had to drink it, because if he did not, and left the country as a live but disparaged exile, he would never again know whether he was thinking or just listening to the rumblings of his stomach.

This fundamental a choice in values escapes most of us today but not all of us. In a midwestern state which passed a loyalty oath law, I knew two philosophers teaching in state schools who were faced with it. One resigned, despite desperate financial need because, he said, to sign it would be to renounce any future rights to speak as a philosopher on political issues. Parenthetically, I should add that he was a man of unimpeachable character, with top military intelligence clearances and a good war record. The other philosopher in the story also rejected the oath, but in a totally different way. He said it was nothing but a statement to the effect that he wanted to receive his paycheck, and so, to take no chances, he signed it, not just once, but three times: bottom, side, and back!

People face the same issues outside the ivory tower and sometimes clearly. A prominent New York lawyer was once retained as counsel for a manufacturer. He had a good salary, a nearly unlimited expense account, and relatively little legal work to do. The manufacturer sent him out to Chicago on business, but the business turned out to be that of entertaining all of the Chicago customers. After a week of high living in restaurants and cafés, he returned to New York and resigned. Not because he didn't like it, but because he *did*. As he explained it, "If I lived for one year like that on their money, then I'd have to live like that on *my own* money, and then they'd have me! I just got out while I still could."

You haven't really said anything when you say that a man wants money—everyone does. The crucial point is that a subtle, double shift takes place in the upward skidder's values. Once you allow yourself to do a job you don't like and do it merely because there is a little money in it, something happens. You have to devalue your own product.

No man of ability can live happily with himself while doing work he frankly regards as below his own standard. This is one of the reasons why so few sports contests are thrown. A man who enjoys competing does not want to be a quitter. A pitcher who gives up a hit when he could have struck the batter out feels like a bum. A basketball player who deliberately misses an easy tip-in hates himself. Such a man is his own Judas. There is no pleasure in doing something at all if you know while you are doing it that it is no good, and this is precisely the dilemma of doing poor work for hire.

If by doing good work, you make less money than if

you do poor work, then what is good and what is poor? In order to live with yourself and do less than your best because someone will pay you for doing it, you have to reject the value of your own work. If you consider yourself a jazz man but play rock and roll, you have to say, "So, what if it is corny? The corn is green." If you accept a bribe to lose the game or the title, you have to try to convince yourself that somehow you are really the winner because you got the larger share of the purse.

What is fame? You can't buy money with it. Such rationalizations are essential, because if one admits to doing poor work deliberately, all his training and previous efforts to develop skills appear ridiculous, and if there is anything an ambitious man dislikes it is to admit that he has spent a considerable portion of his life being stupid.

If the skidder were merely an opportunist, this would pose no great problems because he would not respond to the past. But the ambitious skidder must keep a private record of his past in order to assure himself that he's really moving. He has to prove to himself that his life has a clear continuity, and the only demonstrable continuity is in the steady, serial increase of his income. Thus, where he began as an ambitious craftsman, he is now merely a tally clerk.

If you devalue your products, about the only thing you have left to value about your work is the money you get from it. Perhaps, like the commercial musician on a jam session or the symphony slave playing chamber music on his off hours, you can perform some cleansing ritual, but this takes a lot of extra effort, and money-makers are usually too busy and too tired. The boss or the customer sees to that. The net result is that all you have to show for your fatigue, and frustration, and boredom is the paycheck, and this is an open-ended kind of reward.

In most lines of work that are worth doing, there is a kind of end-point. You can only paint a wall just so well; you can only sharpen a knife to a certain degree of edge; you can only mow a lawn to a rather determinate degree of smoothness. Not so with a paycheck. You can never be satisfied, because there is no absolute standard against which it can be judged. It can always, in theory at least, be a little bigger. The result of this is that now you no longer possess the paycheck, it possesses you.

Then, in many subtle ways your life pattern changes. Just *having* an income is not enough, you have to *use* the income. Using the income means raising your consumption standards. You have to wear a different kind of clothes; you have to drink a different brand of liquor; you have to drive a different make of car; you have to support a different political party, and join a different church. Possibly you can fool yourself for a time with the notion that you are merely doing this by way of advertising yourself to the right people. You're putting up a front that you don't really believe in; you are just making contacts and exploiting a tax-deductible expense account. You are "using" the new kinds of opportunities which open up to you. But in trying to do this you soon satiate your usual hungers, and in order to more effectively use your new affluence you find that you must revise your tastes.

Once you have given up your own standards of craftsmanship, the only index of personal integrity you have left is your tastes; but at this point, Madison Avenue has you for sure, because in moving upward you are no longer permitted autonomy of tastes, if indeed you ever were. When you find your appetites are insufficient and you no longer have any tastes of your own, there are plenty of people ready to provide them for you. And when the competition in consumption reaches dizzy heights, there is always someone to hand you oxygen—at a price.

The drive for success is not just a working out of divine providence for the elect nor the operation of the self-made man slugging his individual way up from the bottom. It is a systematic, commercially profitable tour, planned and carried out by experts, and carrying these same experts along with it. Every bit as much as the kind of poverty-engendered social problems which the Marxists used to decry, upward skidding is the result of the "logic of the situation."

It is interesting to observe the delaying tactics which some people who are aware of what is happening try to employ along the way. One frequent gambit is the double goal. "I'm going to work at this job for just five years, and bank every dime I get. Then I'll thumb my nose at the whole crowd of them and go do what I want to do." Usually, in five years he will have forgotten what it was he wanted to do, and his current tastes will not include thumbing his nose at anybody. Another tactic we could call the broken shoelace gambit. A man sells out all down the line except for one small, symbolic protest, usually in a very safe area. A bright young sociologist who came from lower-class background recently joined a big, commercial, research firm. They saw him as a diamond in the rough, and they have spent a lot of time polishing him. He used to dress like a bum. Now he wears expensive, well-cut suits, good shoes, and neat, conservative ties. But he rarely has his hair cut. This little protest is safe, because if anyone ever comments seriously about it, he can plead that he has just been too busy to get to the barbershop. Another man I know of chews tobacco in his private office. There are a lot of these broken shoelaces, but for the most part they don't show. Private, subtle protests of this sort go largely unnoticed. In time, one way or another, most of the subtle protesters manage to "conquer temptation by yielding to it." They usually call it "maturing."

Not all protests are subtle. Upward skidding scares some people so much they get out of the game. And of course, not all upward mobility is skidding. There are even a few people who systematically employ the double goal and maintain their integrity. Albert Schweitzer and Paderewski both managed this, and there are others. Just getting older in a stable society often produces a degree of mobility which may be absorbed without psychic disruption. The thing that characterizes the skidder and sharply differentiates him from the man who is merely moving upward is his selfless commitment to the ideal of mobility. The skidder is a zealot who will sacrifice everything he thinks he once held dear to the god of success. Instead of a candle burning at both ends, he would be a skyrocket gloriously advertising his own destruction. Show business, professional athletics, and the advertising agencies all provide excellent examples, but they can be found in medicine, law, and the other professions as well. Judged from sheer external appearances the upward skidders appear to be successful. It is only when you know what the personal costs have been that you recognize them as successful failures.

Somewhere in *Plainville, U.S.A.,* James West notes that only a couple of men in this small midwestern community moved all the way through the local class system in their lifetimes.[1] One man went from bottom to top and another did what was equally difficult, going all the way from top to bottom. Skidding is partly a matter of circumstance and partly a matter of talent, regardless of which way you skid. Some people have opportunity thrust upon them; in fact some people get

[1] James West (Carl Withers), *Plainville, U.S.A.* (New York: Columbia University Press, 1945.).

more opportunities than they can stand. A chaplain in Italy in World War II refused a promotion because it meant leaving the front lines. Steinbeck details how the possession of property upset Danny of *Tortilla Flat*. One of my students told me about a lower-class man whom he knew who came into some money and bought a new Buick convertible. Two weeks later he got drunk, poured gasoline over it, and burned it because owning it was separating him from his friends.

Trying to keep one foot in each neighborhood is one of the worst kind of splits. The tragi-comic effort of Jiggs to maintain a dual identification with two divergent reference groups is repeated over and over in our society. You don't have to be an immigrant from a foreign shore to become a marginal man. All you have to do is move from one part of town to another.

The true skidder knows all this and breaks clean. He never slams a door; he just slides out of it with a smile and no salty, backward looks. He knows that you must not be seen with losers. Anyone who maintains *status quo* is on the treadmill and not the escalator.

The automatic value shift is obviously a component, sometimes a major one, in the phenomenon commonly called professional jealousy. When we have ceased to enjoy what we are doing and only enjoy what we get for doing it, we look with annoyance at anyone else who seems to be getting more for doing less. It is significant that we call it professional jealousy and not professional envy, because envy means *I begrudge you what you own and I want,* while jealousy means *I begrudge you what I already consider rightfully mine.* After all, if I have sacrificed everything, I should be paid everything in return.

A sociologist once warned me never to become an expert at something I didn't like. What he apparently meant was not that one should never develop skills outside his immediate, special interests, but rather that the possession of any skill brings the temptation to purvey it, and it might be too expensive to refuse to do something if you could do it well enough, even though doing it was intrinsically unpleasant. He knew intimately whereof he spoke, because he had developed marketable skills in a branch of sociology he really did not care about, but he could not afford to take a lesser job in his preferred area. Happily, he eventually found a good job in his own field, but only after ten years of work, and worry, and frustration. It is not just the musician who is frustrated by the old saw, *He who pays the piper calls the tune.* Anyone who needs money is vulnerable, and this means almost all of us in present-day society. The fact that we can so easily be convinced that we need just a little bit more is the real hobgoblin. And the value shift will get you if you don't watch out. The next time someone tells you that an old friend of yours has hit the skids, perhaps you had better ask which way.

Same
Old Jazz

IS JAZZ A FOLK-ART?[*]

Jazz, that most American of all music, presents a number of paradoxes which excite frequent and often vehement arguments among both its detractors and its adherents. One of these concerns the status of jazz as a folk-art. This writer takes the weasel position that it both is and isn't, but he takes the stand that it is not folkish in the ways in which most writers think it is and that its true folk qualities are largely unheralded and unrecognized.

The terms folk and folkways are familiar concepts to sociologists. They have revered ancestry in usage by people like Wundt, Lazarus, and Steinthal, who studied folk-psychology or what today we would call culture and personality, and William Graham Sumner, whose classic *Folkways* established for all time both the meaning and significance of this term. In seeking some device with which to measure culture, numerous scholars have independently discerned continua between diametrically opposite types, ranging from the small, intimate, isolated and homogeneous community to the large, formal, accessible, and heterogeneous. Robert Redfield calls these two polar types the "folk society" and the "urban." Although other sociologists may prefer different terminology, *viz.*, sacred-secular, gemeinschaft-gesellschaft, status-contract, all readily understand the meanings and the logic behind them.

* Originally printed in *New York Folklore Quarterly* (Winter, 1956).

Folk, folks, folkish, folksy, and folkways all carry certain connotations: primarily, a homogeneity of genetic and ethnic background, and secondly, a uniformity of character and disposition permitting ready and accurate prediction of behavior on the part of peers. "They are our kind of folks." They lack pretention and have a kind of rude honesty about the roles one takes and the use or disuse of social graces. "He's just plain home-folks." They are traditionally oriented and have a time-sanctified social code, plus a storehouse of wit, philosophy, technical advice and metaphysics. All of these are transmitted and diffused by word of mouth and frequently contain diametrically contradictory principles, stated with equally epigrammatic force and bound together by the single tie of long common ownership. "Folks hereabouts have always done it thisaway."

This core of meanings is not accepted only by sociologists. In opening the 1956 seminars on American music at Cooperstown, Carlton Sprague Smith divided music into three broad groups, folk, urban, and art music. He further asserted that, generally, folk music resembled urban music of a few generations previous. In this most sociologists would concur. The city tends to be the center of culture and the locus of innovations. These then radiate to the surrounding areas where, if sufficiently isolated, they may become embalmed, often to the detriment of the arts but to the joy of later culturologists who can find a nearly pure lode of culture long since worn out and discarded in the more accessible urban areas.

Although I agree with these definitions, I disagree right here: Jazz is not a rural music, but characteristically urban. It is not basically committed to the preservation of the past but instead tries ostentatiously to outdate itself daily. While many jazz musicians come from the country, often the "big-foot country," they discard their

folkish ways as fast as they can and strenuously dissemble urbanity in dress, speech, bearing, and tastes.

At the very time that urban bred middle-class boys
go to college and major in folk-lore and prowl the
countryside attempting to collect some hitherto unpub-
lished version of "Barbara Allen," which they will then
sing in Burl Ives tones, there are small town boys who
set out for the city with their beat-up, second-hand
horns. For them the main stream of American music is
not Elizabethan balladry, winding its dwindling way
down to Colvin Hollow, but the blues, moaned or blown
in the cotton fields, mixed with gin and sin on Rampart
and Bourbon Streets, broadcast in a million one-night
stands in dance halls and theatres all over the land, and
now trained, polished, and implemented at Juilliard,
Eastman, and North Texas State College. No falsetto-
singing, modal-chord-strumming, nostalgia-pulling "folk
bit" for them. They want to cut out on the rural scene
and dig what's making on the street.

As far as I can tell, the only thing that country life
every contributed to the art of jazz was to make the
music man so unhappy that he had to moan, so bitter
that he had to shout, and so very glad to get to the city
that he laughed and jumped for joy. Not that the city
was kind. Like other natural forces, the city neither rewards nor punishes; it merely reacts. And inexorably,
many a talented migrant has been debauched, ground
up, destroyed by the impact of urban demands and
temptations on a sensitive personality who had only
ruralways to go on. But for the sake of the art, the
point still must be made: even if the city destroyed these
men, at least it listened, and the country never did.
Otherwise they would have stayed. Art for art's sake is
laudable, but it does not buy bread, and the two main
attractions the city has always held for the jazz man are

music and bread. The larger the city, the more and better of both.

But there is another part to this paradox: the jazz man goes *to* the city; he is not necessarily nor even typically born there. Good jazz men all know this. Listen to any discussion about who blows good horn and where. Like as not the boys will agree on some of the big names, but each will add, "But you ought to hear Bobby Cohn in Cincinnati or Johnny Phillips in Pekin." They know that there are literally hundreds of top-notch musicians who still live in the hinterlands, who have never gone to the big towns, or who never come back. Jazz is where you find it. You often find it languishing in the small towns, but you almost never find it in the hills and hollows.

Another misunderstanding centers on the folkishness of jazz technique. It seems to be true that the early jazz sounds that were played on instruments were fashioned in part after previous vocal sounds. A man first plays what he has heard. Only later does he find a sound which is really his own. But this does not mean that jazz stopped back there. The idea that a jazz musician should be musically ignorant has long since been discredited. Today it is the folksinging kids who can't play a guitar out of the key of E without a capo. The jazzmen know their horns. Granting that jazzmen heavily favor the flat keys (band instruments feel "left handed" in sharps), the man who can't blow in all twelve keys is properly ashamed of it.

We can't defend this next point, yet we must state it: instrumentalists usually suspect that vocalists are not really musicians. Practically all jazz musicians are instrumentalists, while most folk music in America leans on the lyrics. Many a modern jazzman of stature is a college or conservatory graduate himself. He does not *collect* music like a folklorist; he creates it. Jazz today is a living, changing art. The people who are making it are urban, sometimes even urbane. They are trained and literate instrumentalists and composers and skilled improvisers, which is really just another word for a fast thinking composer who blows his horn well. They live in the city; they work in the city; they feel with the city when they feel anything other than their art. They may be refugees from the swamp lands, but their feet are clean and they wear shoes. They are trained, intent, knowledgeable and sophisticated, and they are critical about what they are doing. Folksy they are not.

Despite all this, there is a kind of folk quality about jazz, although professional folklorists are not likely to find it. Collecting folklore of any sort demands that the collector establish rapport with his folk. Anyone who has done field work knows well enough how difficult this can be. The researcher is rarely even *from* the people, much less one *of* the people, and they know it. If he has the right informal credentials, a congenial personality and some friends in the area, he may bit by bit be admitted, but it is often slow going. The more different his ways and background, the less trustworthy his data. If he is white and the people he is interested in are American Negroes, the wall is nearly impenetrable. Even if he is a Negro, but urban and educated, the wall is still there. Willis James recounts an episode in which he was trying to study the music of an isolated Negro community. As a college professor, he had to struggle to gain a little confidence. Why was he there? Was he an investigator of some sort? Did he want to ridicule their ways? What good reason could he have to come to them? At long last a man gave him one sardonic lyric:

> Listen what I tell you
> Understand me well
> Strangers ain't welcome here
> Home folks is catchin' hell!

This underlines the problem of research among the really primitive grass-rooters of jazz. Long used to subjugation and exploitation, these people cannily avoid any commitment as long as they can, and if they must talk with the researcher in order not to be rude, they try to figure out what kind of answer he wants and then give it to him. Usually the answer is a kind of double talk which simultaneously says to all the real people around them: "Look here at this man. What is he up to anyway? Let's give him a pleasant answer and maybe he'll go away." Under these circumstances, the old jazz musician will agree that he was once on such-and-such a band and that he probably heard such-and-such a tune twenty years before it came out. In fact he will agree to almost anything, because he doesn't really care. Many current myths in jazz apparently arose in just this way. Some of these myths are gradually being dispelled.

The research problem today is more complex, because the musician is more sophisticated, but it remains similar. Musicians, like folk people, are intensely loyal to their own kind, and although they are obviously urban, they are in peculiar and deliberate ways isolated. They do not fear to talk with people. They will pass the time of day with anyone. They appear to the stranger affable and casual, but also shallow and superficial. This is largely just a blind, serving the same purpose as the "Yas, suh, boss!" of the old southern Negro. There is one prominent saxophonist whom I know from whom I have never been able to get one word of criticism about another musician's playing. It is not, I am sure, that he is not critical. The excellence of his own performance gives the lie to this. His affability is a cover; he does not trust me. I might air his critical comments in an article like this one and thereby make him the center of controversy which he does not seek. He much prefers to go on just playing good jazz.

This does not characterize all jazz musicians. Some of them are violent personalities and vocal about their dislikes. But the jazzman today is often in the public eye. To eat he must get along. It is easier to get along if you don't let people get too close to you. So he often cultivates an easy front that goes about two inches deep and he keeps private his real feelings. These he shares only with other musicians and close friends who have proven that they can be trusted.

The jazzman then does have the folk characteristics of intimacy, and isolation, and group loyalty. He also has the unwritten code of conduct which he has learned in the only way it can be learned, by firsthand participation. Marshall Stearns reports how this even cuts across national boundaries. A foreign newspaperman who was a jazz fan suppressed a good story because it could have caused embarrassment to the Gillespie band on their Middle East tour.

Another characteristic of folk people is a cultivation of various delicious brands of private humor. These are meaningful only within the group and they are often expressed in language which defies translation into other tongues. The jazzman's world abounds with such humor. Jazzmen also have their own John Henrys and Mike Finks about whom all manner of enormous lies are told. In fairness, some of the lies are true.

But while the language is obscure and personal, it is not characteristically archaic. In much linguistic research among folk people in the United States, we can find traces of Elizabethan or other early literature. Isolation and illiteracy add their typical errors in transmission, but isolation restricts innovation. But jazz, being urban, thrives on invention and change, and the language of the jazzman moves like the hand on the keyboard, twisting the words, changing them, re-combining them, and discarding them when familiarity reduces their freshness of impact.

At any point there is a jargon. In the swing era, it was called jive talk. Jive referred generally to the kidding, self-consciously phoney mannerisms which the jazzman affected, both in his personal behavior and in his music. A great jazzman summed it up when he said: "There's nothing wrong with jive, as long as you know it's jive." Unhappily, at all periods there have been those who forgot, and there have always been outsiders who never knew. The language of the jazz group is always full of jive, partly drawn from the storehouse of folk-wit which the jazzman brought with him in his trek to the city, partly coined on the spot to express an immediate need, much of it found haphazardly in sheer experimentation with words. But very little of it is really poetic. The language is in general ambiguous, impoverished, and insignificant. The real core of the jazzman's subculture is the music. All else is superficial to it, coming and going like flotsam on the sturdy fluid wave. You don't have to have a special haircut to play good horn; you merely get the haircut to look like other musicians. Talking the current slang does not give you the beat. All of this is just jive.

A final similarity to folk music lies in the content of the soloist's improvisations. While the ideal of the improviser is a completely fresh and original melody, most melodies are actually constructed from bits and snatches of previous ones, patched together and unified so that they are, in a sense, original but in another sense strongly imitative. There are few great original talents in jazz. Nearly everyone shows the influence not only of specific musicians, but also of the time and cultural milieu in which he learned to improvise. Just as the folk ballad singer borrows verses from other ballads to shore up his own, so also does the improviser borrow "licks," "riffs," and other small segments to add sparkle and continuity to his own personal ideas. To copy whole someone else's chorus is either a mark of great adulation (particularly when this chorus has already become famous on a record and would be immediately recognized by all sophisticates), or else it is a cheap and deceitful way of feigning an ability to improvise which is actually lacking. But to borrow a useful measure here or there is merely regarded as common sense and good taste.

To sum up, jazz does have its roots in folk music, especially in the blues. And these roots go deep. Probably twenty percent of the music played at the 1956 Newport Jazz Festival was frankly blues, all kinds of blues, including *Green Blues*. But it did not sound much like Bessie or Cow Cow or Leadbelly. The roots lie there, strong and deep, but the tree keeps branching upward into more rarefied air all the time. The connection between the early blues singer and the contemporary West Coaster is more than just a tenuous, aesthetic one. Both are members, though of different years, in a warm fraternity of kindred spirits. To the jazzman, other jazzmen are home folks, although he will likely disdain the word. The main qualities in which the jazzman resembles the folk artists of another time are in his sincerity, his playing mainly for himself and his friends, his suspicion of strangers, and above all his deep and abiding conviction that he must follow his music where it leads him because it reflects the essence of his life.

SOCIOLOGICAL NOTES ON THE JAM SESSION*

Most jazzmen agree that no one can understand jazz or jazzmen except jazzmen themselves. This, in turn, becomes understandable when we recognize that jazzmen exhibit a cult-like consensus on certain esthetic matters, employ an esoteric jargon, and are usually neither trained nor disposed to seek similarities between their ways of living and those of other persons. Indeed, many of their peculiar characteristics can be traced to the fact that their contacts with outsiders, when not restricted or actually prohibited, are distorted into limited patterns.

Accordingly, a thorough investigation of jazzmen demands that one be both jazzman and social scientist: some musical competence is necessary in order to gain entree and to establish rapport; some social science background is necessary in order to abstract and generalize accurately about the behavior observed. I began playing dance music for money and jazz for pleasure in 1939 and have played one or the other ever since. Although I attained salable competence on three instruments, I have never made music my principal means of livelihood; I am what professionals call a Saturday

* Reprinted from *Social Forces* (Vol. 33, No. 2, December 1954) by permission. Copyright, 1954, by the University of North Carolina Press.

night musician. My friends and fellow musicians, however, have included a great many professionals varying
in age, experience, and prestige, so that my data were
drawn from a broad sample of observations. These
were discussed and verified by two former graduate students, both of whom were alumni of big-name bands.[1]

The jam session is a recreational rather than a vocational activity of jazz musicians. Not all dance musicians
are jazzmen, although the typical employment of the
jazzman is in a dance band since this is the nearest commercial compromise available.[2]

Dance music is music for dancing, especially ball-
room dancing. Jazz is better defined as an art form
rather than in terms of social utility, but it is exceedingly
difficult to define verbally the characteristics of an art
which employs non-verbal means of communication.
Suffice it to say that jazz is a kind of musicians' music,
played for the enjoyment of musicians and a few other
persons who participate in it vicariously. Although some
jazz creeps into a dance band performance, much of it
is played not for the general public but semi-privately,
and its most characteristic occasion is the session.

The jam session is a transitory, recreation association
of an elite. It is an informal but traditionally structured
association of a small number of self-selected musicians
who come together for the primary purpose of playing
music which they choose purely in accordance with
their own esthetic standards, and without regard for

[1] I am pleased to record my gratitude to Bertram Gardner
and Vernon Michaux, whose observations and insights com-
plemented and clarified my own.

[2] H. S. Becker has analyzed some of the vocational problems of the musician. It should be said that Becker's analysis
applies more precisely to jazz musicians than to dance musicians
generally. See Howard S. Becker, "The Professional Dance
Musician and His Audience," *American Journal of Sociology*,
57 (1951), pp. 136-144.

the standards of the buying public or of any acknowl-
edged organizational leader or critic.[3] The session frequently takes place after the formal vocational "job,"
and the busman's holiday aspect of this is explained by
the jazzmen as "a chance to get the taste of commercial
music out of my mouth." For outsiders, the intensity
of distate the jazzman feels toward money-making commercial dance music surpasses belief. In a very real
sense, the session is a ritual of purification for him, a
self-cleansing by the reaffirmation of his own esthetic
values.

While this and other meanings of the session are
private to the group, the location is only relatively private. Since most musicians are employed in metropoli-
tan areas, the location is typically urban. While sessions
may occur in a private home on an invitational basis
similar to that of a salon, more of them take place in
the lesser night clubs in the marginal or blighted areas
of the city. The club is chosen with several criteria in
mind: 1. It must be relatively small and obscure to
provide privacy and minimize interference from casual
spectators. 2. Good food and drink must be readily
available. 3. Club hours must be long and flexible because sessions are likely to occur between eleven p.m.
and four a.m. or on Sunday afternoons. Sessions are
impossible in most homes since the neighbors will not
tolerate the noise, and only the occasional wealthy
patron can afford the space, solitude, food, and drink
which the musicians require. 4. It follows that the chief
criterion is a permissive manager, himself frequently a

[3] Becker, *ibid.*, erroneously implies that no social control
exists in the dance band. Informal control exists in all dance
bands, being at a minimum in the "gig" or pickup job where
a band is assembled for only one performance. In large bands,
considerable formal control exists as well. The reaction to the
severity of this control is one of the factors which makes for
the popularity of the session.

former musician. Significantly, mere proximity to job or residence is not very influential; so long as the location is reasonably accessible, jazzmen will congregate. Only a few such clubs are selected in any city and the tradition of sessions at one of these clubs may persist for several years.

Jazzmen deliberately attempt to exclude the general public from the session, and this is facilitated by the after-hours and off-limits setting of the session. The musicians are extremely conscious of their kind— friends are greeted warmly but strangers are viewed, if at all, with critical reserve and condescension. In part this is a reaction from the objectively similar but functionally different professional performances. Any customer who dares request a tune not approved by the musicians or who tries to tip the band—beyond buying a round of drinks—is likely to be told off in highly uninhibited language. The performers, not the spectators, are going to run this show.

A jazzman new to the group usually accompanies a sponsor who considers him acceptable and introduces him to the boys. They ask where he has worked, whom he knows, and if he knows a certain little spaghetti house in L. A. in a general effort to discover mutual friends and background. With more reserve, the same treatment is accorded the jazzman who drops in uninvited. If he gives the right answers he may be asked to sit in, that is, to replace one of the men then playing.[4]

---

[4] The sit-in practice is deplored by union executives, because through this practice, a club hiring four men may have the services of a dozen free if it can tolerate the music produced. Since sitting-in is highly valued by jazzmen, various compromises are made, such as a ruling that the number of men on the stand shall at no time exceed the number called for in the club's contract. Even such rules as this have been dodged by having players standing or seated on the dance floor nearby.

The first three or four tunes the newcomer plays constitute a period of trial and initiation. He is tense and exhilarated because he knows all the others are watching and listening, although they do not appear to be doing so. Both as a gesture of politeness and as a test, he is asked what he would like to play and perhaps in what key. His choice is a password, for to establish himself properly in their eyes he must choose one of about a thousand standard jam tunes, for each of which there are only a few traditional keys. Should he name some tune which is unaccepted, he will be told curtly, "We don't know it." (A lie!) "Let's play 'Rose Room.'" This being the case, he had better play "Rose Room," or whatever, in *their* key, and play it well.

Once the tune is selected, key and tempo are established in an introduction which is played typically by piano but possibly by any instrument or even a combination of several, according to prearrangement. This term "arrangement" requires explanation. Theoretically, jam session music consists of free improvisation around the melodies and harmonies of traditional tunes. Actually, certain introductions, cadenzas, clichés, and ensemble obbligati assume traditional association with specific tunes and come to be viewed as an organic part of the tune itself. These, however, are folkways, informally established, and are sharply distinct from the formally arranged music of the dance band in that they are rarely written down but rather learned from hearing ("head arrangements").

Thus, jam music is not, as naive critics believe, totally unarranged and spontaneous; it is, rather, non-literate. Instruction and inculcation of both the manifest expressions and the norms are thus primary and sacred, rather than secondary or secularized like so much of the technical education of our culture.[5] In other words, the only way one learns these things is by playing at sessions. If the newcomer knows the right tunes, the right keys, and proceeds to demonstrate that he has ability and understands the right way to go about playing them, he thereby proves that he is really a jazzman and not an upstart or intruder. If he is good as a jazzman, he is immediately accepted as a member of the group. If he is admittedly a novice but is eager and humble, he may be tolerated and encouraged. This is more likely to be true if he is young—say, under the age of eighteen. If he fails, he is out.

Two things are simultaneously required of the jazzman on a session: he must subordinate and integrate his musical personality, as expressed through his instrument, into the general group, and he must do this with no score or conductor to guide him. On the other hand, as a soloist, he must produce startingly distinctive sound patterns which are better, if possible, than those played by any other member of the group. How can he do this?

In the introduction, the key and tempo are set. Except by prearrangement, under unusual circumstances, these remain constant for the duration of the number. The "solid" rhythm provides a basic temporal referent which all are obligated to respect.[6] There is another referent, less precisely defined, since it is only approximately conventional and may undergo limited variation. This is the harmonic scheme of the tune, a regular pat-

[5] In recent years some formalization of the process has been attempted through the publication of instruction books on improvisation and Jam Lists of standard tunes and their traditional key. The books usually fail in achieving their purpose, and few musicians carry them.

[6] Because of the importance of solid rhythm, the term "solid" came to be applied to anything good or desirable or approved by the jazzman.

tern of chords of rather definite duration. The Gestalt of the harmonies is constant, but modifications are encouraged so long as they consist of subtle substitutions of nearly equivalent chords, so that the effect is synonymous and not antithetical.

Beyond this, there are no clear-cut rules to guide the performer. He must imagine the pattern in advance from what he hears of those playing around him. He must select a part in this pattern appropriate to the occasion, his instrument, and his personal abilities and liabilities. The same process is carried on by each member of the group. He must not clash with the others nor pre-empt their parts in the pattern. If this collective enterprise succeeds, each feels the full warm response that comes from the wholehearted cooperation of a group. Indeed, such feeling is greatly intensified, because the immediacy of expression possible for a musician who has command of his instrument provides a more profound emotional release than almost any other kind of activity. It certainly provides the supreme emotional experience for the jazzman.

The attempt to be at once traditional and distinctive points up a fascinating paradox which runs throughout all aspects of jazz. Musically, the attempt takes the form of selecting sound patterns as different as possible from the original tune and yet at the same time internally consistent and recognizable (by experts only!) as related to the tune from which the process started. The notion that art is solely the expression of the individual finds no place in the jam session. The soloist must be unique, personal, and "progressive," but in order to meet the other criterion of the esthetic, he must be understood by others who know the idiom. This means, of course, a continual advance into abstraction and esotery, so that contemporary jazz is always musical casuistry, forever seeking new ways to rationalize the impossible.

If the reader perceives the significance of this, it will be obvious why most jazzmen, unschooled in logic and philosophical esthetics, are at a loss to verbalize their aims and methods and resort to jargon (itself unexplained) or else refuse to discuss jazz at all. As far as expressing and communicating their basic ideas to outsiders, jazzmen are not only non-literate but non-verbal as well.

This is the crucial point in explaining the cult-like aspects of jazz. Jazzmen specialize in communicating musically with one another and with the small minority of non-playing listeners who make up the elite group, but they are almost totally unable to translate their most important feelings into more generally conventional symbols. Like the practitioners of various forms of mysticism, they can only converse meaningfully with someone who already understands. This loads the session with all sorts of other latent functions. Here is the occasion for a man to experiment with musical ideas—unrealizable outside the context of the group performance. Here too must he practice the art of ensemble improvisation. Here is where the promising newcomer is trained to carry on the traditions and develop ideas of his own. A man here makes the impression on others which gains him prestige and which ultimately may decide whether he is acceptable on a professional job. Here again each jazzman must reinforce his contacts with all of the others and on each new occasion must test and prove his status, since one bad performance may cost him all that a dozen good ones have gained.[7] He resides somewhere; he works somewhere else; but it is in the session that he most meaningfully lives. This is what he practices and learns for. This is the focus of his life.

[7] Here jazzmen and jazz record collectors differ, the record collector extolling a man for performances that contemporary jazzmen consider out of date and thereby devalued.

One further ramification will be explored: the manner in which norms developed in the course of a particular set of experiences become generalized and applied to others which seem superficially unrelated.

We have seen that the jazzman is isolated from persons in general society in several important ways. His time is organized differently—he sleeps while they work, works while they play, and plays while they sleep. He is 120° out of phase with the workaday world. His art is esoteric and so intimately bound up with performance that few non-performers gain even a remote inkling of its meanings; hence he comes to regard all non-jazzmen with suspicion and looks primarily to other jazzmen for psychological support. The strain toward sophistication within the group requires that he spend most of his time practicing to increase his command of his instrument, since improvisation deteriorates with any lag between conception of an idea and its execution. The technical demands are so great that twenty-four hours a day are hardly sufficient for one to develop and maintain his skill. Many top-flight jazzmen literally carry their horns with them at all times so that they can steal practice time at every opportunity.

Most jazzmen are recruited in their middle or late teens. Talented youngsters may reach the big time before they are eighteen; to do this requires a single-minded concentration found in almost no other group of teen-agers with the possible exception of athletes. While other young people are children, occupationally these youngsters are men. But they are a strange sort of men, since they are in part self-made and they have had little experience in the construction of personalities.

Two facets of this early recruitment are especially significant: the exclusiveness and the revolt. In regard to the latter, adolescence in America is typically a period for critical appraisal of the cultural values and a time to experiment with sacred trusts and forbidden fruits. Radicalisms and idealisms of all sorts make strong appeals to youth. Jazz is at once radical and idealistic and suffused with the glamour of Promethean artistry and the raw vulgarity of the brothel. And, like athletics, it is one of the few fields in which the young actually can achieve a leading role as the quick reward for hard work and personal ability. To become a great jazz artist when one is sixteen is a wonderful way of running away from the triple tyranny of home discipline, school discipline, and financial dependence. It is revolt as a hero, or at least as a martyr, and not as a runaway child.

Staying up all night when other people sleep, talking about things others can not understand, smoking, drinking, spending one's own money, and all the rest of it lead a youngster to grow up fast, at least in some ways. Here lies the importance of the exclusiveness. The young jazzman develops sophistication approaching precocity in one narrow realm while retaining a child-like naiveté in others. With so much effort and time devoted to becoming a skilled technician and artist, he has no time left for learning much of anything else; the few other things his associates care to teach him are largely uncritical violations of the moral standards which have been imposed upon him as a child, at school and at home. Thus he sees in the jazz life a great freedom from the old restrictions, and since his adoption of the new norms is voluntary, he does not perceive that these also may restrict. In short, the only norms he must learn and obey are esthetic norms. Let us briefly examine the nature of the jazz esthetic.

The jazz esthetic is basically a paradox, tragic in that it is ultimately unrealizable. The comprehensibility of traditionalism and the radical originality are irreconcilable. Experimentation is mandatory and formal rules become suspect because they too quickly stereotype and ossify; but personal leadership is transitory and charismatic, because no single successful performance assures permanent prestige. Composition is inferior to the act of composing, as is implied in the standard tunes and their unique interpretation.

There are no dependable rules for constructing a good jazz solo. There are informal pressures, but these usually remain unvoiced. A jazzman virtually never asks or tells a fellow jazzman how he sounds or how he should behave unless the two are unusually intimate. Only subtle hints may be dropped. If a man does not pick them up, he is tolerated if he is good and avoided if he is not. Compliments are given sparingly and usually understated. Discussion of an absent third party may be free and critical and even adulation is not unseemly. But the informal pressures are applied lightly. If much forces is applied it may dissolve the group, and in a small minority, where the members need each other as intensely as jazzmen do, this must be avoided at all costs.

Since jazzmen have largely cast aside the norms learned in childhood, and since they are so strongly devoted to jazz, the esthetic norms of jazz loom large in their thinking and shape their general personality organization and their outlook on moral and political problems outside the field of jazz. The generalization of these peculiar norms results in some striking clashes with the conventions of the general society.

If we inquire about group attitudes toward matters that do not concern jazz, the basic answer must be given that jazzmen are almost exclusively interested in jazz. Little else matters beyond the necessities of existence: such things as food, drink, clothing, and sex. The bond which unites jazzmen is so strong that differences in other things can be ignored. It is this which fosters the widely recognized tolerance of jazzmen toward race, religion, and class. Some do-gooders naively believe that a jazzman's tolerance is a high-minded fellow-feeling. It is fellow-feeling, but it does not stem from the kind of high-mindedness they seek. The jazzman tolerates these differences because they do not matter. It is easy to be tolerant in areas where one does not care, and the only thing he cares about seriously is jazz. Thus tolerance extends to homosexuals, wife-beaters, schizophrenics, draft-dodgers, alcoholics, drug addicts, and what-have-you, if only they are jazzmen. And no special stigma attaches to "characters" who are not, since by definition all non-jazzmen are "squares" and one is hardly worse than another.

Lacking a clear-cut superego himself, the jazzman expects other people to be strange and shrugs it off. One widely experienced sax man impressed the writer with his coolness in critical situations. When asked about this, he replied, "I've learned to expect anything from anybody at any time." He sees social life as unstructured and takes only a self-centered interest in it. He is hedonistic; he lives for "kicks," principally in music but, by extension, in sex, food, alcohol, drugs, and various unusual experiences. Personal eccentricities of all sorts are regarded with tolerant amusement as long as they do not interfere with the music.

Political attitudes were neatly summed up by a trumpet man during World War II: "Just let me blow, man. Just let me blow."

In brief, the intense and early specialization of the jazzman, who enters this cult in his late teens, prevents him from participating in the norms of the general society.[8] Finding his values flouted by outsiders, he retreats further into the group of those who understand.

[8] An alternative hypothesis is that jazzmen are somehow selected for their peculiarities of personal behavior and social attitudes. This will not be analyzed here because of the complexity of data and discussion it entails.

Since he receives his chief emotional satisfaction from
this group, he dares not criticize it and thus refrains
from making the normative judgments outsiders would
make on the members' behavior. Identifying with jazzmen, he perceives the outside world itself as disorgan-
ized and crude and worthy of no respect. At the same
time, the paradoxical demands of the group ideals and
the conflicts between commercially profitable dance
music and esthetically satisfying jazz become almost intolerable, so that he must develop a sort of controlled
schizophrenia, an ability alternately to care or not care
about what he is doing. If he fails to make this tenuous
adjustment, he may easily become seriously disorgan-
ized, but his neurotic or anti-social behavior will itself
be tolerated by group members so long as it does not
impede progress toward their principal goal—the production of jazz.

Author's note: The ten years which have passed since
this article was written have brought three notable
changes. First of all, quite a few jazz musicians are
now at least superficially conversant with problems of
esthetics, and with the development of university
course and degree programs in jazz, the trend will continue. Secondly, experiments have been made with jazz
in non-binary rhythms. Most first-rate performers can
now swing smoothly in ¾ time and a few can manage
occasional performances in times based on five and
seven. Finally, the current trend in improvisation is
away from chords as such and aims at development
rooted to themes and artificial scales. This trend has
not progressed sufficiently for me to evaluate it at the
present time.

Let's
Get Cosmic

IN THIS CORNER...

Liberals and conservatives misjudge each other in characteristic ways, partly because of the different means and methods which they employ and partly because of differences in the criteria by which they judge. Rationality is the essence of the liberal's image of man. He considers man a logical, self-directing organism. Thus he thinks that man is most man-like when he is most intellectual. Not that the liberal is unemotional, far from it. What arouses his emotions to a pitch of ecstasy is a beautifully presented, logical argument supporting an original view in such a way (he thinks) that no intelligent, reasoning human being could remain unconvinced. He really believes the old Greek adage about the identity of "the good, the true, and the beautiful," and also that "you shall know the truth and the truth shall set you free." Hence, he is concerned about the logical and ideological purity of his stand. He fears that he may someday be inconsistent, and he is compelled to back up his words with actions lest his friends accuse him of being merely a "talking liberal." (It is freely assumed that *all* liberals talk, so we need only observe who acts!)

The conservative's main criterion is predictability or, as he sees it, dependability. The most conservative of modern men are accountants, whose books must *always* balance. Sound money, unequivocal roles and statuses, orderly processes, constitutional government, respectful ritual are, for the conservative, the highest achievements of man. The beauty of regularity swells his breast with dignified, paternal pride. Folklore supports him at least as well as it does the liberal: "Don't change horses in the middle of the stream"; "Don't rock the boat"; "A bird in the hand is worth two in the bush"; "The mills of the Gods grind slowly, but exceedingly fine." The conservative is no Prometheus *chained* to a rock; he has built his house upon one.

The liberal interprets the conservative's disinclination for argument as intellectual weakness. He thinks the conservative is stupid or uninformed. Obviously, says the liberal, if a man is intelligent, he questions; and if he questions, he argues and experiments; and if he knows he is right, he proclaims and defends. On the other side, the conservative regards the liberal as irresponsible. How else can he account for the liberal's carping challenge of all of man's most sacred achievements, the discounting of order so painfully wrought and so necessary to predictable behavior; the liberal's cavalier eagerness to risk current, practical advantages in pursuit of some golden dream with dubious prospects of material realization. John Dewey phrased this well:

> Let us admit the case of the conservative; if once we start thinking no one can guarantee where we shall come out, except that many objects, ends, and institutions are doomed. Every thinker puts some portion of an apparently stable world in peril and no one can wholly predict what will emerge in its place.[1]

Liberals view change as potential progress; conservatives view change as probable disaster. Most liberals love to argue for the sheer fun of it, and many do not

[1] *Intelligence in the Modern World,* ed. Joseph Ratner (New York: Modern Library, 1939) p. v.

even keep score. When conservatives argue, it is usually because they have been goaded into it by liberals, and often it is merely that they are being conventionally polite. They would rather tell the liberal to shut up, but this is not seemly. In public controversy, it is easier to find liberal than conservative spokesmen, if one wishes to stage a debate. Debate usually makes the conservative uncomfortable; to the liberal, it is one of the joys of life.

To simplify, we may say that intellectualism tends to be associated with liberalism and power with conservatism. With minor disclaimers this is true, and it is not just empirically true; it is logically necessary. Our institutions almost automatically support the relationship between conservatism and power. Whereas a poor man can go broke easily, it takes calculated action for a rich man to do so. The stability of society is also his stability, and if he does nothing but put his money into government bonds, he can't lose. With a broad range of other investments, he is almost bound to win. To financial power, we automatically add political power and social prestige. If you start with enough power, you must be a fool to lose it. Moreover, if you start with enough, there is little incentive to try too hard for more; you tend to make only safe investments, to gamble only on sure things, to buy only when you can set the price.

Thus the man with sufficient means rides along on inflations and actually gets richer during recessions, when circumstances permit him to buy in at a bargain. The really powerful man is often very pleasant socially and well known for his good works. He can afford to be. A man who has or can get almost anything he wants and shows ill-temper is sick. The security of power makes for placidity, and thus the conservative model of personality becomes one of studied deliberation, even meditation, but hardly intellectual conflict. The typical man of power is not easily swayed by someone else's arguments, and he has little need to present arguments of his own. He has, for him, more economical ways of convincing other people to do his will, should they need convincing. If you have it, the cheapest thing in the world is money.

When we recognize the identity of personal power and the power of society, perhaps we should applaud the conservatism of most men of great power. A yapping, irresponsible fox terrier can be kicked out of the way, but a neurotic Great Dane could destroy us! Some of the giants who have been irresponsible have done nearly as much damage to society as good. Since he is rarely an intellectual, the man of power is better advised to be a conservative, because while he will make few improvements in society he will at least do it little harm.

If power makes a man conservative, intellect tends to make him liberal. By intellect here I mean more than a high I.Q. or a university degree. I mean the active or even chronic use of the mental faculties. A man who thinks, as opposed to one who meditates, must constantly seek new things to think about and new ways to think about them. An Alexander can cry when he sees no more worlds to conquer, and his despair is echoed by every intellectual who is "between engagements" with problems. Intellectuals do not commit suicide while they are working on problems but after they have solved them. Sherlock Holmes needed Watson's needle only when there was no crime to solve.

Thinking is an active and exploratory process and not the telling of ancient beads, however sacred they may be. The intellectual, whether professional or amateur, performs two essential functions; description and evaluation. The lifelong operation of the scientist is to describe the world around him, whereas the architect and engineer try to change it and the businessman works to exchange it at a profit.

Evaluation takes the form of justification or criticism. Justification is the style of people who have become addicted to intellectualism somewhat inadvertently and would perfer to kick the habit altogether if they could. Explorers who have drifted into the real estate business, artists who have become rich, middle-class opponents of the Crown who have gotten knighted, philosophers who have become fashionable—all of these become justifiers. Perhaps the best example of a justifier of all time was Thomas Hobbes, but many another will do.

For the intellectual who has no personal interests at stake, evaluation is automatically criticism. When the intellectual becomes a critic, he usually becomes a liberal, too. This useful function which the intellectual performs for society does not often endear him to it; but societies, like animals, die when they cease to change, and social changes are abetted by intellectual criticism. Thus for the most part, the men of great power and the intellectuals are at odds, since the one must of necessity demand change and the other must oppose it. If society were taken over by critical intellectuals, it would probably be torn asunder, and in the overly-protective arms of powerful conservatives it would likely smother.

Both liberals and conservatives suffer from the confusion of means and ends which Gordon Allport called "the functional autonomy of motives." They start by supporting certain ends, which in the process of achievement seem to them to demand certain means. If the means work, they are repeated. There are many old sayings attesting the stability of habit structures which work: "You can't teach an old dog new tricks"; "Nothing succeeds like success"; "The good adjustment is the enemy of the better," and so on. However, since B. Zeigarnik's[2] classic experiment about the effect on memory of interrupting tasks before completion, we know that sometimes unfulfilled ends may be just as intensely pursued. After using a given set of means over a period of years, we tend to feel that these are the only methods of getting anything done.

Really committed liberals and conservatives dogmatically and doggedly pursue ends, which in the nature of things may never be achieved. The long continued pursuit leads them to over-prepare their chosen means, with the result that even when the ends are achieved, they tend to go on employing the means. The difference lies in the choice of means. Liberals think in terms of change and jar us by looking for arguments to win, exposés to publish, bridges to blow up. Conservatives respond to dignified order and bore us with solemn processions, pontifical pronouncements, and self-righteous declarations of unity. Both kinds of behavior seem, on close inspection, to be directed largely from the lumbar, rather than the cranial, nerve centers.

If we examine the morality of the two positions, both show flaws which a lawyer would attack under the laws of property and the laws of persons. Put another way, liberals are frequently materially irresponsible and conservatives are frequently inhumane. Liberals are usually willing to spend money (especially someone else's money) to save people, whether they know the people or not. Indeed, not knowing them may be an advantage, as the history of the European refugee problem has

---

[2] Zeigarnik, B. "Uber das Behalten von erledigten und unerledigten handlungen," *Psychologische Forschung,* 1927, IX, 1-85. This famous experiment is mentioned in many textbooks and discussed extensively by Kurt Lewin in his *Field Theory in Social Science* and in *Dynamic Theory of Personality.* "Zeigarnik effect" or "Zeigarnik quotient" are common terms today.

shown. On the other hand, conservatives are often ready
to spend people (and this of course nearly always means
young and draftable people) to save property, sometimes even if it is not yet their own property. Liberals
consider people to be sacred, as conservatives consider
property. Thus each thinks that the other's willingness
to sacrifice is unholy waste. Modern warfare, which
consumes property and persons alike, can be pretty
rough on both.

In peace time, the legislative liberal seeks human
rights and the legislative conservative seeks property
rights. Socially, the liberal wants to be loved and ad-
mired whereas the conservative prefers to be respected
and obeyed. Both liberals and conservatives are concerned with property, and with people, but they have
different intentions. Conservatives generally approve the
way property is currently distributed, whereas liberals
want to change the rules and manner of distribution in
order to favor groups not currently propertied. Thus
a political opportunist may appear to be a liberal while
he is fighting his way up and appear to become a conservative once he nears the top. This has happened on
a wide scale in a variety of historical settings, as history
has often been made by opportunists.

This apparent change of ideology should not be
taken to imply that the opportunist in his liberal phase
does not seek power or that in his conservative phase
he does not revel in it and seek to gain more. He rather
changes his mode of getting it, and once he enjoys
success he reveres the institutional support of power as
the best means of maintaining and increasing it. For
example, after 1832 the English bourgeoisie got a political foothold from which to defend the economic
advantages they had originally wrested from society by
ingenuity, opportunism, personal risk, and sheer luck.
In short, first they got the money; later they added the

political power with which to conserve it. This direction of development is not inevitable, as other historic examples show, but the point is that a man tends to become conservative when he obtains something worth conserving.

Another instructive example is found in the history of patent laws and the changing attitude of the big corporations toward them. The change was a result of growth. Small entrepreneurs trying to get started were the worst sort of patent pirates, but as private agreements and patent pools permitted the development of major corporations, the attitude toward infringement changed and clever use of the patent laws became a major tool of development, every bit as important as financing and research. It should be noted that most private inventors were equally disgusted at both phases. In phase one, Eli Whitney became so disenchanted that he ceased to make use of patents altogether. In phase two, a number of inventors complained that they wasted half their lives in the courtroom. In either case, the men who built the large corporations were usually anti-intellectual opportunists who exploited the inventors and scientists or else stole from them outright. The lesson is pretty obvious: few real intellectuals are either equipped or motivated to profit much personally from the kinds of social changes which their ideas help to produce. The man who profits in such times of change is rarely committed to anything but himself, and he must be a man who can change his ideology as readily as his shirts.

The epithets which liberals and conservatives conventionally hurl at each other affect neither very much. The conservative rarely believes that pure ideas are necessary in order to gain practical results. He is no logic chopper. "A foolish consistency is the hobgoblin of small minds." What counts most with him is not intellectual persuasion but power. "I teach my son to be rich." "My country—may she always be right—but right or wrong, my country." For the conservative, the counterpart of the good, the true, and the beautiful is the honorable, the dignified, and the solvent. He likes what he sees and he regards dreams, like Scrooge's ghosts, as undigested mutton. The liberal can really hurt the conservative not by proving him illogical or unimaginative but by making him feel ridiculous. Laughter is the foe of solemnity, and the weakness of the conservative is the fear that, like the fabled Emperor, he may appear in public in transparent clothes.

As for the liberal, loss of dignity does not faze him; he cares little for clothes. Overalls, G.I. shoes, or loin cloths are more or less one, useful but hardly important. He is so often used to nakedness and indignity that he secretly suspects even himself when he acquires the attire of affluence and position. What he fears most is not being undignified but being absurd. His Achilles' heel is in his syllogisms. The conservative cannot insult him by charging that he is irresponsible; this is an accolade to his courage. He is not hurt when conservatives complain that he is improper; he knows he is forthright and frank. What he fears most is that he may be shown to be illogical, that his calculations may be fallacious, that his reasoning may be proved wrong. He can afford to be funny but he cannot afford to be morally inconsistent, or illogical, or factually incorrect.

The liberal thinks that originality of expression, quick repartee, and the ability to think on one's feet indicate intellectual vigor and entitle one to leadership. The conservative thinks that power and position which have been attained are in themselves sufficient proof of intelligence and any further display of brilliance is undignified, unnecessary, immodest, and dangerous. Liberals think conservatives are smug and stuffy and conservatives think liberals are flippant and brash. Most of the time, both are correct.

Thus the most effective detractors of conservatives are the satirists, humorists, and comedians. Will Rogers, Franklin D. Roosevelt, and Mort Sahl have dealt telling blows in defacing the self-images conservatives have so carefully built. The most effective conservative controls over liberals are usually applied privately, through bureaucracies, boards, and the decisions of carefully composed committees, but if the conservative wishes to wound the liberal in public it is best done with precise, spare, formal logic.

If the satirist and humorist are the preferred champions of the liberal, the conservative could choose an impeccable lawyer or Jesuit priest. Sometimes such choices are made, but most of the time neither liberals nor conservatives strike where they should, and each parries the other's blows.

If one is interested in concrete results rather than rhetorical exercises, different tactics should be employed. The liberal who wants to change things should not alarm the conservative and should never affront him. He should salute all the flags, attend all the banquets, bow to all the gods. He should never criticize a structure when he can modify its functions instead. He should avoid discussions of basic principles and seek agreement on specific actions. He should guard his language so that at all times he appears to be "practical." He should keep his best jokes to himself, since the essence of most humor is disorder and disrespect. He should be solid, stolid, and solemn, and at times a little obsequious, all the while supporting the conservative's emotional need for order. "He should keep his trousers pressed."

For the conservative, the advice is almost the reverse. He should freely entertain criticisms of the structure.

This does not mean he must constantly change it; often all the liberal really wants is to be heard! He should willingly agree to form committees. He can probably get his people on them. If not, it will be some time before they report, if they ever do. He should appeal to the liberal's philosophical principles and not argue implementation. He should appeal with simple logic and in quiet, unemotional tones, with no vibrato in his voice and no grandiloquent references to our grand and glorious heritage, or the rock of ages, or our unswerving loyalties. Admittedly this is difficult for the conservative, because verbal obeisances are part of his life, but he, like the liberal, must learn that you cannot always say things your way if you want others to hear you. Since the liberal respects critical intellect, the conservative should pretend to be an intellectual and a dispassionate critic. Above all, he should never pull rank or stand upon his dignity but should present an image of humble, informal reasonableness. He should display a sense of humor. He should be cheerful. He should reward the liberal's emotional needs for progress and change.

This advice to each to dissemble the other is not as easy to effect as it may sound. When a conservative tries to behave like a liberal, he too often becomes loud and rhetorical, and liberals call him reactionary, hypocritical, and a demagogue. When the liberal tries to simulate the conservative, he often becomes so obviously quiet and close-mouthed that conservatives think he is organizing a conspiracy. It takes skill and perseverence to bring it off, but the advice is tested and sound nonetheless. You can do liberal things in a conservative way and conservative things in a liberal way, depending on the climate and the times. This is one of the basic secrets of political success.

I have said that the liberal prizes discussion, and that the conservative respects affirmation, but it is the appearance, and not the reality, which each accepts. Both are symbolic, and wise men see them as such. Unwise conservatives regard unwillingness to affirm as defection, while unwise liberals regard requests to affirm as a slur on their character. Naive liberals regard refusals to discuss as proof that the opponent lacks intellectual integrity or that he has no case. Naive conservatives regard invitation to discuss as attack.

When two groups of people do not communicate— or even associate, as is often the situation between liberals and conservatives, they tend to suspect each other's motives and to think the others are plotting against them. And, in their ignorance of the other's activities, they may exaggerate the scope and organization of the opposition. There are interesting differences in the language with which they express their fears. Extreme liberals fear compact alliances of great power interests bent on brain washing and the suppression of information and freedom. (The fact that many media of communication are controlled by conservative interests lends credence to this fear, but actually the conservatives are not that much interested in what people think and say, since they see so little purpose is discussion.) Extreme conservatives, on the other hand, fear seizure of power and a sudden replacement of personnel, perhaps even by assassination, sabotage, or widespread violence, and they suspect liberals of plotting infiltrations to pervert the sacred institutions they need to trust. Take, for example, the left-wing polemics against power structures, such as those by C. Wright Mills, and the right-wing alarms about insidious conspiracies sounded by the John Birch society. In each case, a little truth is made to go a long way because the facts are fugitive and to the extreme liberal or conservative, much of the important data about the other side is always unavailable.

Both sides do a great deal of transvaluating. Each regards the very terms of "liberal" and "conservative" as hortatory and pejorative, but they disagree about which is which. This is why real conspirators in our society do not argue with those whom they seek to infiltrate. To the liberal camp they are "fighting liberals" and to the conservative they are "ultra-conservative." Ironically, the fears each camp has about the other are partly true; that is to say, there are dangerous people in each. The weakness is that neither conservatives nor liberals scrutinize their own cohorts as closely as they do those on the lunatic fringe of the other side.

American conservatives, who were quick to spot a homosexual entrusted with military secrets in the liberal ranks, failed to regard Senator McCarthy as psychologically disturbed. Our friends are never alcoholic, they merely enjoy their liquor. Our friends are never homosexual, merely sensitive aesthetes, if men, and strong, vigorous personalities, if women. The ironies of these imprecise and inverted definitions have often been pointed out by comedians. Recall W. C. Fields' delicious line: "A man who hates children and dogs can't be *all* bad!" We just have to face the fact that there are some nasty conservatives and some nasty liberals. No one is much more offensive than the kind of liberal who dogmatically hates everyone who hates and insists on being on the minority side of every issue, although the snobbishly, ultra-correct conservative does run him a close second.

Conservatives are mistaken when they see all liberals as dangerous conspirators. Crane Brinton points out that a frequent forerunner of revolution is what he terms the "desertion of the intellectuals." The intellectual, as I have pointed out, must either justify or criticize. By "desertion" Brinton means that few intellectuals are justifying and most are criticizing; when this happens, the intellectuals are actually formulating in more precise language what is already felt by the masses. It may appear to the conservative that the intellectuals are leading the revolt or that they have in fact started it. This is almost never true; they give it words and music. Intellectuals, of course, provide words and music for all sorts of social dramas, but most of these shows never get on the road. Far greater changes in society flow unintended from changes in technology than follow the exhortations of political or economic reformers.

Most reformers are voices crying in the wilderness. Their words are seldom heard, or if heard, seldom heeded. Only when people are ready to move will they learn slogans and quote editorials, often slogans and editorials which were written a generation before. There are few revolutions or even minor reforms which cannot claim a long and distinguished intellectual ancestry, but this hardly proves that these earlier intellectuals were prophets, let alone leaders.

On the other hand, liberals overestimate the ability of conservatives to kill ideas and control thought. Any worthwhile idea will occur to many different men. It is an egotistical interpretation of history which has made us regard great thinkers as something special and unusual. Not only do many men have the same ideas at different times, but many of these ideas are so commonplace that most men do not even bother to write them down, and only when some scribbler with less perspective or greater personal ambition commits them to print do they appear in a form which historians can date and document. Some of the most facile Johnsons have had no Boswells, which may be regrettable but has probably not impeded the movement of the world. What man has thought, man can think again, if circumstances merit. The logic of history is as stern with the ambitions of the conservative as it is with those of the liberal. You can't keep a good, or even a bad, idea down; but ideas are only part of the world and not the essence of it.

It may seem from this discussion that liberals always consciously operate from logic and conservatives always rest on tradition. Far from it, each feels that he is logical and each regards his position as the traditionally acceptable one. Logic and tradition are, in actuality, only the forms of presentation in which their respective ideas are congenially cast. Both liberals and conservatives actually lean heavily on intuition and both fall short of their avowed models. No one who reasons clearly and understands tradition can possibly desire to preserve everything in his culture or, on the other hand, to change it all. Both change and order are utilitarian and both are required. The problem is to know when to preserve and when to change, and the great danger is that once we have defined ourselves as liberals or conservatives we feel obliged to live up to the label.

Thus it is that many liberals are trapped into assuming that the latest idea is the best one and that being old automatically means being old-fashioned. The caution observed by scientists in their presentations makes it probable that a newly reported scientific discovery is already aged in the academic wood, well tested, and likely to be sound. However, when flouridation and the Salk vaccine were first announced, many liberals jumped on the bandwagon and clamored loudly for the adoption of these measures without the slightest comprehension of the evidence in their favor. These appear to have been happy choices, but many others have not been.

Conservatives for their part are often correct in their reluctance to indulge in half-baked experiments. But while reserve protects the conservative against foolish or naive innovations, it traps him into not only retaining old and tested procedures, but preserving old and unnecessary risks as well.

Educators, even in psychology and education departments, use worn out procedures in teaching their students, even when the content of their teaching itself proclaims the need of change. In economic life, high profits have been justified classically by high risks, but many businesses (the utilities are a cogent example) pretend that high risks still exist in order to justify high profits when the risk-taking has long since disappeared or has been shifted to the price a consumer pays. Conservative refusal to plan land use or the regulation of resources, because this seems somehow to invade the free enterprise system, causes untold waste and hardship and increases the costs of existence for all, conservatives and liberals alike. Where natural resources such as oil and timber are specifically concerned, it is, ironically, often the liberal who attempts to conserve and the conservative who is most irresponsibly free in his destruction, exploitation, and profligate waste.

While it is reasonable to assert that men of considerable power tend to be conservative, it is not as simple to explain conservatism in men of lesser position, who might be thought of as having much to gain from change. The conservatism of small men greatly distressed Karl Marx, who tried to explain it as "false class consciousness."

The fact that modern corporate structure has a conservative influence on individual personality has often been noted by William H. Whyte and others, but the full meaning of this influence has not always been made clear. Conformity means predictability and the interchangeability of parts, and this functional sameness, or interchangeability, is as necessary to corporate finance as it is to the manufacture of repeating rifles. The loving care of the old gunsmith may be emotionally appealing, but Winchester turns out more arms. Organization men must be conservative in order to be interchangeable and they are apt to be so even when they think they are being most original. Nothing is more ludicrous to a truly independent thinker than the highly contrived ritual of brainstorming in which the official cheerleader cries out: "All together now, boys—think different!"

Real liberals do not, in fact, make good organization men, even when organization is needed to attain their objectives. When originality, ingenuity, and inventive talent are necessary, as was true in war-time intelligence and propaganda efforts, some queer fish are dredged up; and order and organization suffer. Free thinkers are just that: free, unbound, often unbound even by their own voluntary discipline. As a result, useful application of their plans must almost invariably be made by someone else. The liberal who is, by necessity, critical of the existing structure and, by virtue of his freedom from commitment to current routines, able to be inventive, is also by his very originality often unable to leave anything alone long enough for him or anyone else to profit from it. Someone has to pry the idea away from the innovator before he takes it apart again. This does not apply merely to political or economic liberals but to liberals in all fields. Many inventors of mechanical objects are also like this. David Buick was said to have made fortunes for at least fifty other men though he died poor. He just would not leave an invention alone. Ironically, he left his name on a car which became the very badge of conservatism!

Both conservatism and liberalism have side effects; a conservative or liberal role, especially in one's occupation, tends to color other roles in which there is neither logical necessity nor social pressure toward consistency. In other words, occupational style tends to set the whole style of life. For example, accountants tend to be conservative Republicans, whereas social workers tend to be liberal Democrats. If one prizes his ideological position, he must be wary in selecting his vocation. In some fluid situations, a liberal finds himself handed power and becomes absorbed in a complex organization for which and to which he then becomes responsible. Becoming part of the structure often leads him to give up criticizing it. It may be this as much as anything else which leads a man who is liberal as a youth to become conservative in his old age.

Conservativism and liberalism have many functions in our society. Beyond the obvious bows we make to balance of power when we are in a peacemaking mood, there is a subtle, psychological function which these positions serve which I like to call the "icon roles." In the long run, this function may be the most significant effect of both conservatism and liberalism, and many of the apparently direct, practical results may derive indirectly from the psychological.

The first analysis of this kind which I know is Veblen's classic, if sardonic, defense of conspicuous waste as a needed challenge to a society bent on increasing production. Conservatives and liberals portray for us on a many-levelled stage the basic questions which we must ask ourselves whenever our actions are voluntary. Shall I act in the same old way, or is there a better, new one? Americans laud inventors such as Edison and Fulton, but most of their money goes into the pockets of experts in repetitive processes whose names we never hear until they run afoul of the anti-trust laws.

In nearly every field, the best paid jobs are those whose intrinsic fascination has long been reduced to an intellectually dull but intensely profitable routine. The most fascinating part of medicine is research but more profits go to the hardworking practitioners routinely diagnosing known diseases and prescribing penicillin and aspirin. Electronic engineering can be exciting but it is usually limited to polishing standard circuits to see if some component can be omitted from the new model. I have been told that an engineer who can figure out how to eliminate one or two resisters from a T.V. set will thereby pay his salary for the year! To be sure, some large concerns have their Steinmetz, happily ensconced in his own private laboratory, but the justification of his pleasure—in the long run—is their profit. Architects enjoy their dreams, but realtors make more money. Jazz musicians get their kicks but Lombardo is better paid.

W. I. Thomas once said that all of man's desires could be reduced to four: the wish for security, the wish for new experiences, the wish for response (by which he meant personal friendship and affection), and the wish for recognition. The conservative acts out for us the desire for security, and the liberal acts out the desire for new experiences. The conservative is our God of Winter, and the liberal our God of Spring. We know what we are and how we are acting by reference to them.

There are liberal and conservative eras: that is, there are periods of time, often very brief, in which one model or the other catches the public fancy. Young people who are coming of age intellectually at these times often commit themselves to one or the other view, and with the resolve which the pleasures of identification and the pains of subsequent conflict induce, some do not modify this basic commitment as long as they live. Thus it is that people who came of age in the 1920's or in the 1950's are typically political conservatives, while those who came of age in between are more frequently liberals. The great icon of the 1930's was, of course, F.D.R. and whether he was experimental or not, whether he was intellectual or not—in fact, if we must, whether liberal or not—he convinced the great majority of thinking youth that to be a liberal was to be a good man. How they shocked their parents, and how shocked they were, in turn, to see their children follow the conservative icon, Eisenhower! Clearly we cannot always transmit these profound faiths to our children.

If we perceive the symbolic function of the liberal and the conservative, we see that each needs to keep a sample of the other around. Each is the other's pole star, even though he prefers to steer south. How could we be sure that President Kennedy is a liberal if it were not for Senator Goldwater? This is why the most stable conservative college faculty needs its tame liberal. On the state occasions when the faculty either fictitiously or actually deliberates, here is the man who can be counted on to shock us by the radicalism of his views and thereby assure us that the move we are about to make is really a very conservative one indeed. And when, on the other hand, liberals timidly propose some advance which they know is a lukewarm compromise of the bold principles they wish they could stand up for, the tame conservative comes to their rescue. By his grudging and reluctant aquiescence in this modest revision, he assures them that it must be really very bold and very liberal indeed. Each helps the other know who he is. For most liberals and conservatives, the other camp is like New York City, a fine place to visit but not to live in. Of course there are also those really encrusted conservatives and liberals who don't dare make even a passing acquaintance in the other camp and content themselves with vicarious images of the other obtained from the pages of the *New Republic* or the *Chicago Tribune!*

In different language and with no more consistent results, we Americans are as anxious as the Russians about our ideological stands. Will Rogers archly observed that communism was about one-third practice and two-thirds explanation. We have no dialectical materialism, but we have both liberal and conservative ruts. To get any action for the public good accepted, we must convince ourselves that it is at once both conservative and liberal. The truth is that the liberal's position, like the conservative's, is a radical oversimplication of life and serves to assure him that he can see his way through the morass of problems which continually beckon and which individual intellect is inadequate to assess.

Intoning either liturgy is like going to church, and different people prefer different churches. And just as most church-goers are abysmally ignorant of theology, most so-called liberals and conservatives have only the dimmest notions of what their respective positions really entail. For small-scale liberals and conservatives, the differences are mostly a matter of which icons they bow to and how they sing the hymns.

PEOPLE, THINGS,
AND IDEAS

There has been a wealth of argument recently about man's place in a world of machines. Teaching machines, thinking machines, and automatic factories invade areas once considered sacred to man. The synthetic juxtaposition of mechanically produced sounds threatens to displace the composer, and electronic translation of language is within view. Yet a righteous clamor surrounded the home run record of the great Babe Ruth, and those who threatened it were regarded as Titans by some and thieves by others for daring to challenge his highest mark. As vast areas of our lives are handed over to the authority of non-human forces, we become more grimly concerned with maintaining personal autonomy over other areas, but with no general agreement as to which areas are which.

We expect artists to interpret life for us yet we deplore any picture we can't immediately understand. When the portrait photographer forgets to kick the tripod as he takes our picture, we complain that it doesn't look like us, when in reality the trouble is that it does. We are ravenous for ideas, devouring psycho-analysis, philosophy, and economics, frantically searching for answers but not pausing long enough to formulate our questions. We have become so involved in subtleties that we have lost sight of any bold outlines of intellectual order. We need a clear understanding of some basic categories into which we can sort our world, and some notion about the proper relationships between them.

Categories do not come ready made; man himself constructs them. There can be as many as his imagination affords and his leisure permits. Kant played with this question, as did many another philosopher, and no two of them completely agreed. If we back off from the problem a little, however, we can see that there are three items which are irreducible in the process of man's thinking. There is man himself who does the thinking. On this point, Descartes took his famous stand. Secondly, there are the "things," all the objects in the world. Third, there are the thoughts which man develops in the process of contemplating himself and his surroundings, his ideas. These three elements are essential to any intellectualizing. Someone to think, something to think about, and the thought which links the thinker and his object.

Three important categories in our world, then, are people, things, and ideas. They are obviously different, and it may seem naive or tendentious to argue that people should be treated as people, ideas as ideas, and things as things. However, these are not the only possible ways to treat them. In fact, very often things are treated as if they were people, people get treated as if they were things, and so on. The possibilities of treatment may be arranged in a table, as on page 156.

We should note that for each right cell in this table there are two wrong ones, and this theoretical diversity may be empirically observed today. The confusions which result from treating these categories inappropriately are traditional in our culture and thus in our personalities, with myriad, unhappy results.

In discussing the personality, William James pointed

TREATMENT

CATEGORY	People	Things	Ideas
People	people as people	people as things (people as tools)	people as ideas (the party of the first part)
Things	things as people (corporation)	things as things	things as ideas (monuments and amplifiers)
Ideas	ideas as people (icon roles)	ideas as things (fetishism)	ideas as ideas

out what he called the "material self," by which he meant that we identify ourselves with our personal possessions. "Clothes make the man," to say nothing of the woman. The army recruit is told that he salutes the uniform, not the man inside. When we wish to note some deed of heroism, we pin a medal on the man who did it, as if we couldn't tell a hero from a coward without a medal. We have made a kind of folk figure of the woman who tries to ward off depression by shopping for a new hat. Such women usually wear, or at least carry, gloves. This is how you can tell the lady from the sales girl: the lady, like a naval officer on formal inspection, wears white gloves, while the clerk, like the swabby, is bare-handed. And while men may laugh at the woman shopper and try to avoid being clothes horses themselves, they act out their own materialistic charade with their automobiles. They do not so much drive their cars as support them. In fact, the material notion of the self is nowhere more clearly shown than

in the illegal oversimplifications of the juvenile delin-
quent, who steals primarily the conventional symbols
of personality. Boys steal clothing, guns, sports equipment, and automobiles; girls steal cosmetics, jewelry,
and clothes. In each case, they steal what their culture
has taught them to cherish. We even use the body itself
as a badge of identification: haircuts, hairdos, and
beards become marks of status. In all of these ways,
we look upon ourselves as things, identifying ourselves
with material objects.

Even more obvious are the ways in which we treat
other people as things, regarding them either as means
or as obstacles to our own personal ends. The compulsive, hard-driving boss regards his secretary as a tool,
like the filing cabinet, or the switchboard, or the Veri-
fax machine. He accepts her demands for coffee breaks
as he accepts the periodic cleaning and overhaul of the
typewriters: an inconvenience to be budgeted under
maintenance. However, such casual and impersonal disregard is sheer philanthropy compared to the attitudes
of the early entrepreneurs in the cotton mills and, more
recently, in the movies and TV, in which female workers
have been regarded at times as the manager's harem.
The radio performer Gene Shepard characterized one
TV station as "an electronic bawdy-house." Kinsey gave
the ultimate *coup de grace* to any illusions of romance
which might be cherished about sexual unions when he
termed them sexual outlets. His manner is only a little
less chilling than the brisk way in which military men
write off selected troops in an engagement as expend-
ables. We are often merely things to ourselves and
probably we are merely things to other people most of
the time.

On the other hand, we treat things as people. Since
Roman times we have formed the language of law in
personalistic metaphors. A corporation is literally an

embodiment, that is to say, a kind of Frankenstein's monster which has practically all of the rights of a person with none of his mortal limitations. John Jones *versus* General Motors is more of a mismatch than David and Goliath because, as Biblical history assures us, Goliath could be killed. General Motors can't. Old corporations never die; they just recapitalize and merge. In religion, many primitives indulge in animism, and many critics think that the rest of us do, too. The fetishism of *The Glass Menagerie* is part and parcel of our own lives. Plato wrote about prisoners who looked at shadows on the wall and thought them real. Modern electronics has replaced his poetic image with a concrete object, the omnipresent TV. Let us note ambivalently that modern television "talent" is now too professional, too sophisticated in the projection of selected shadows, to slip into self-exposure like the prototype Uncle Don of early day radio.

The general semanticists have accused us of forgetting the differences between abstract and concrete aspects of reality. We sometimes treat people as ideas. The lawyer who views his client as an interesting case which might serve to establish a legal precedent and the psychiatrist who sees both patients and friends as diagnostic categories are equally guilty of a depersonalizing kind of abstraction. More to be censored, no doubt, is the politician who thinks always in terms of "my constituents" or the egoistic entertainer who is always graciously presenting himself to "my public," and trampling over real people in the process. Those who love humanity and hate individual people are really at one with those who fall in love with love. If people are not like their ideas of people, so much the worse for people.

It is difficult for us even to recognize that we treat ideas as if they were people. The personalistic metaphor in our society was reinforced by our recent past as a rural or folk society in which most events, abilities, resources, and possibilities were intimately bound up in concrete corporate individuals. Power meant Man-power, and machines were at best an extension or ampli-fication of human energy. In a town hall meeting, the individual voter was a force to reckon with. The con-tracts for assistance which one created informally with his immediate fellow men were his chief source of pro-tection against mischance and disaster.

None of this is fundamental today. Natural energy from sources other than man does most of our work. The machines are so standardized that any one of thousands of men can run them, and thus even the operating skills of individual men have been de-individu-ated. Most operations need not involve human skill or decision at all; once constructed and set in motion, our finest machines operate without human direction, requiring men only for their occasional therapy. The town hall model of politics is totally unrealistic, and even the image of City Hall is fast becoming obsolete. Perhaps *you* can't beat City Hall but Washington lobbies can. Insurance has replaced friends, and today the criterion of a good neighbor is one who keeps his nose out of your business.

And yet, with all these changes, we cling almost des-perately to a personalistic manner. We call each other by first names, long before any ceremony of *tutoyer* has authorized us to do so. This gets pretty funny when we call each other by the *wrong* first names, as we often do. We tell intimate little ancedotes to casual strangers to reassure ourselves that the world is full of friends. Over our cash registers, we post little cards reading "A stranger is a friend I have not met." This chummy man-nerism is a last-ditch effort to conceal the fact that much of the time we are not dealing with real persons at all but merely with human beings who act out the part of some idea. Other societies do this also, but without all the self-accusing ritual of denial. The Barong in Bali is known to be activated by men. The Hopi Kachinas are masks donned by people from the tribe. The Mask with which the primitive Nigerian depicts his values is known by him to be a mask, transubstantiated only for the duration of the ritual. But we Americans are less sure and are unwilling to admit both that we need fairy tales and also that we think our fairy tales are true. We try to act as if we treated every person we meet as a living flesh and blood friend, refusing to admit that the very people to whom we ascribe the greatest importance are not behaving as people at all but merely acting out roles, lending their bodies to depict ideas.

All you need to do to test this assertion is to imagine some important person behaving like a human being. Imagine a judge laughing in court or a movie glamour girl belching, or the President of the United States scratching himself. It is downright indecent, because ideas are not supposed to itch. Thus the man who portrays them must deny that he does.

Most of the famous people I know of seem to be famous not for what they are but for what they represent. They serve as icons exemplifying one or another abstract concept of virtue. To assuage our soldiers' loneliness we have pin-up girls who advertise something which is not for sale. These same soldiers serve us all as heroes who play the role of bravery, often through accident, desperation, or in some cases psychopathic inability to fear. In peacetime we observe a continuous pageant of sports, with a rapid succession of college athletes, each loudly cheered as he disports himself in the arena and each in turn promptly forgotten. These young men play for us the concept of vigor, and youth, and manliness, and it is with mixed feelings that we view the better technical proficiency of a balding Bob Cousey, Sam Snead, or a flabby Archie Moore.

Veblen understood these icon roles well, although he had other terms for them, referring to conspicuous waste and conspicuous leisure. The finest example of conspicuous leisure, perhaps, was the Mandarin with his long fingernails which proclaimed for all to see that he could afford to be absolutely useless. We chide the citizens governed by limited monarchies about their figureheads, but we have our own figurines, in the "good union man" and the "ambassador of good will." If we stop to reflect, we see that the vast, complex division of labor of a modern society ultimately makes effigies of us all.

Our culture is so admittedly materialistic that we can dispense with any serious argument to prove the point and merely indicate some examples of our over-materialism. For instance, you can invent a thing and patent it, but it is harder to patent a process, and a mere idea is not patentable at all. Comedians call a short comedy sketch a "bit" and this concrete term is now extended to all kinds of events. The entrepreneur degrades his own ideas and inspirations by saying "Oh, yes, I have a couple of *things* going." The fierce acquisition of objects of art among many members of the upper- and middle-class is a kind of conspicuous consumption documented by social critics from Veblen to David Riesman. The average man cannot play at high stakes, but he collects tools in the basement to convince himself that he has constructive talents or he posts decals on his windshield to prove he has seen Death Valley. Would-be scholars make a fetish of surrounding themselves physically with books they may never look at and would-be housewives collect recipes. All of these things are chips which are played in the game, but the house

tricks us with a kind of inflation called planned obso-
lescence, so that so long as we play we cannot win.
In case it seems that this essay is a plea for Zen
Buddhism or some other psychological Soma, let me
suggest that the recent Beat revolt was merely a transvaluation of the materialism of middle-class society.
Operating with a self-imposed restriction of materials
does not necessarily make one philosophical. It is more
often only a *tour de force*, like writing a novel without
using the letter E. Our society has so materialized ideas
that even our language makes it difficult to talk of ideas
in any other fashion, and S. I. Hayakawa tells us that
when we wish to understand each other's ideas, we must
ultimately point at things.

The confusions of things as ideas and ideas as things
are so pervasive in our society that it is hard to distinguish them in analytic writing. We have treated concepts
as if they were words for so long and dollar bills, poker
chips, and other conventional coins as if they had intrinsic value that we can hardly admit it could be a
confusion. A fine place to observe the confusion of treating things as if they were ideas is in that supposed storehouse and shrine of ideas, the American college. Colleges want a campus which looks like a picture postcard
and most of them employ photographers who can give
even the worst collection of outworn rubble a postcard
look for the catalog and other advertising blurbs. Winding walks suggest leisure, and for the speculative wander-
ings of Socrates and the other peripatetic philosophers,
we substitute the meaningless, physical wandering of
students and faculty alike. Just wandering around without sound ideas has often had disastrous results. The
Wandervögel of Germany are one case in point. We
yearly don academic garb recalling a hallowed past, but
we no longer teach or study that past. We grant degrees
wholesale, but we discount thought in the process. Some

schools still grant their degrees in Latin to students who are not even literate in English.

The ultimate in teaching efficiency, we are told, is not a teacher at all but a teaching machine. The efficiency is not debatable, but the image calls to mind Rossum's Universal Robots. Too often we mistake the thing we can see for the idea we say we seek. How can you tell if a boy is a student? Just count his courses. How can you tell if a teacher is a scholar? Just count his books. How can you tell if a teacher is a coach? Just look at the record of his teams. An I.B.M. machine is not Einstein nor a tenor sax Lester Young.

If there is anything to our boasts about the superiority of this civilization over those which have preceded it, we ought to order our lives in such a fashion as to make ideas serve people and things serve ideas. Only fools defend the dignity of things. I recall when I was about ten years old, walking in upper Manhattan with my father when we passed an old cemetery. In it was a large monument, and by that time I had been conditioned to the use of monuments to mark historic sites, so I asked my father who was buried there. He said he didn't know. I looked back speculatively, fearing to miss something important, and said, "Well, gee, he must have been important to have such a big stone." My father gazed thoughtfully for a moment and said, "I'll tell you. The way I look at it, if a man is really important, he doesn't need a big stone because people will look for his grave; and if he isn't important, a big monument just makes him look silly."

The pretentiousness of monuments to the living and to the dead is basically snobbism, and snobs usually prize things over people. Some snobs buy highly pedigreed dogs in order vicariously to deny their own mongrel ancestors and most snobs wear badges of some sort. I'll never forget the shock I got once when teaching evening school at the University of Cincinnati. The course was Introduction to Western Civilization, one of those pretentious potpourris which no teacher less able than Da Vinci can really manage. I was struggling nightly to encompass the scope of more information than I understood when a couple came up after class and announced to me in solemn tones that they "were people who appreciated the finer things in life." While I have thought of many witty replies subsequently, some of them cheerily obscene, at the moment I was completely dumb. As I reflect on it, the whole problem is summed up in their one line. They appreciated the finer *things*. Not people, not even ideas, but just the damned things.

As time passes and more and more artifacts are made, things coerce people and grind them down. Things contest with us everywhere for space. You can't reason with them, you have to walk around them. The placement of telephones, hallways, or other means of access and communication subtly but inexorably determines the social structure. Some people use these ecological principles but most of us just get used by them. In the service of phoney ideas about aesthetics, we have developed some of the most dysfunctional objects any culture has ever produced. Our automobiles are too low for comfort, hang emptily over the wheels at both ends, and include vast, expensive panoramas of glass which are as impractical as a picture window in a bathroom. Any engineer in the business will tell you that you can't get the manufacturer to spend an extra twenty dollars to put in a really durable transmission or to improve the frame, but he will freely dispense a hundred dollars worth of chrome and other worthless ornamentation or reshape the fenders to make sure that the sixty-three model is distinguishable from the sixty-two.

When we look at the work of architects and realtors,

the situation is worse. It is hard to choose between the ills of unplanned cities and those which architects deliberately plan. Here again, the trouble is that the realtor doesn't give a damn about people or ideas; he only wants money, and the architect is trying to find a gimmick which will provide a trademark. Who cares how the people feel who live there? At one of the best architectural schools in the country, I saw a young man painstakingly drawing a huge beehive of hexagons. I asked what he was up to. He said he was making a module, so that he could more easily design hexagonal houses. When I asked why he wanted to, he did not understand my question. The answer was self-evident to him—no one else was doing it. Thank God!

To all the harassed six-footers in low cars, the half-size ladies looking for chic dresses, the left-handed students at right-handed desks, the broken-legged residents of split level houses, and the average man-in-the-street who is shoved, dirtied, frightened, and continuously abused by the material monsters of our vaunted civilization, I say, "*People* of the World, Unite . . . !"

The battle is joined but it is far too early to predict the outcome. Some people are beginning to regard tools merely as tools, although this may be more due to economic pressure than to philosophy. The publication of paperback books is a good start. They serve ideas just as well as the more traditional hard-shells, and at less expense of money, time, and space. Miraculously, readers appear to agree. The widespread use of plastic materials is also laudable, even though it occasionally miscarries. Of course, both the plastic containers and the flimsy books may merely denote a frantic transiency instead of the implementation of fundamental values.

There are also some current developments which are reactionary or plainly wrong. The use of hard boxes for cigarettes is wasteful and ridiculous. Most people are as well off with a cheaper soft pack. It may be a plain waste of time even to discuss the relative merits of cigarette packages, if the whole business of smoking is basically wrong. Elijah Jordan used to say "There can be no morality in an immoral situation and there can be no rationality in an irrational situation." Few Americans are as fundamental as this, and they soberly debate the efficacy of various cigarette filters reducing the probability of cancer, instead of just quitting smoking altogether. Why? Because about the only way most Americans have of asserting the presence, let alone the importance of the person, is through participation in extreme sensations or kicks. After the callousing abrasion of material objects and the sense-deadening clamor of commerce-serving sounds, it takes a pretty severe jolt to make the average man feel he is still alive. The jolt is found in Spillane, Kerouac, The Untouchables, Gunsmoke, benzedrine, stock-car races, frantic vacation trips to gawk at the Grand Canyon and the Yellowstone bears, and the continuous fume of adulterated cigarettes and the accompanying scald of badly brewed coffee.

And yet, through it all, the American keeps looking for yardsticks to measure what he has. He reads Kinsey, hoping to find a method of keeping score on his sexual activity. He secretly hopes that he can break par, but secretly fears double-bogie. He buys hi-fi equipment by reading the catalog specifications. Having learned that cars are to be judged by horsepower, he quickly learns that amplifiers are rated in watts. Obviously, the more the better. Manufacturers are quick to oblige. They now make and sell amplifiers which produce 140 watts for living room use. To anyone who knows anything about audio, this is wild. An amplifier which delivers an honest 60 watts can be used for public address at football games. If anyone ever turned 140 watts of sound into a reasonably efficient speaker in a small closed living room it would shatter material objects and do physical damage to people. But just wait. Next year we'll top ourselves with 200 watt amplifiers which will cost twice as much and obviously must be twice as good. The fi keeps getting higher, or at least something does.

There is no way to deny the charge; our civilization is pretty sick. And the basic trouble is that our value system is wrong. Fundamental confusions have obliterated our understanding of the proper relationships of people, things, and ideas. We need to develop a true functionalism, and this does not mean we should go out and buy a batch of ugly, naked-looking furniture. We must start by gaining a clear and broad understanding of function. We need a reasoned, consistent theory of the relations of people, things, and ideas.

It is useless to rush about trying to patch up our institutions, passing laws, establishing fly-by-night investigating committees to straighten this thing out before the end of the fiscal year. We need a sober reappraisal of our whole value system, because all actions imply values, and there is no way to assure sensible actions unless we know what our values are.

SELECTED READINGS

The books listed below are all pertinent to the ideas presented in the previous essays, some of them to ideas set forth in several of the essays. They have been chosen with two criteria in mind: significance and readability. By significance, I mean their usefulness to the college student who is trying to define his own place in our complex society. All of these books raise questions, and a few of them help provide a basis for answers. They vary widely in content and style, but most of them are readable, even entertaining. The list is intentionally short in the hope that the books might actually be read. Paperback editions are noted where known.

Brinton, Crane, *The Anatomy of Revolution*. New York: W. W. Norton & Company, Inc., 1938 (available as Vintage V44).

Chase, Stuart, *The Proper Study of Mankind*. New York: Harper and Brothers Publishers, 1956 (available as Harvest HB 26).

Conger, George Perrigo, *The Ideologies of Religion*. New York: Round Table Press, Inc., 1940.

DeGré, Gerard, *Society and Ideology*. New York: Columbia University Bookstore (Distributor), 1943.

Graves, Robert, and Hodge, Alan, *The Reader Over Your Shoulder*. New York: The Macmillan Company, 1944 (available as 47 Macmillan).

Greenwood, Ernest, *Experimental Sociology*. New York: King's Crown Press, 1945.

Jahoda, Marie, Deutsch, Morton and Cook, Stuart W., *Research Methods in Social Relations*. New York: The Dryden Press, 1951.

Jordan, Elijah, *Forms of Individuality*. Indianapolis: Progress Publishing Co., 1927.

Miller, Harry L., *The Ways of Mankind*. Chicago: The Center for the Study of Liberal Education for Adults, 1953.

Muller, Herbert J., *The Uses of the Past*. New York: The Oxford Press, Inc., 1952 (available as Mentor Ms. 112).

Rogers, Carl Ransom, *Client-Centered Therapy*. Boston: Houghton Mifflin, 1951.

Sapir, Edward, *Language*. New York: Harcourt Brace and Company, Inc., 1921 (available as Harvest Books HB 7).

Stearns, Marshall Winslow, *The Story of Jazz*. New York: Oxford University Press, 1956 (available as Mentor MD 240).

White, Leslie A., *The Science of Culture*. New York: Farrar, Strauss, 1949 (available as Evergreen E 105).

Whitehead, Alfred North, *The Aims of Education*. New York: The Macmillan Company, 1929 (available as Mentor M 41).

Whyte, William Hollingsworth, *The Organization Man*. New York: Simon and Schuster, 1956 (available as Anchor A 117).